WARM-UP IN FOOTBALL

Every football training session and match should begin with a warm-up in order to improve performance and reduce the risk of injuries.

Warm-up in Football provides scientific evidence for the effect of warming up and describes how performance is closely related to muscle temperature. Furthermore, the book explains how the right warm-up prior to a match and at halftime improves the outcome in football.

This book provides a basic understanding of the value of warming up and presents a significant number of warm-up programs that can be used whether you are training professional, amateur or youth players. The warm-up programs and exercises are tailored to different training and match situations both on and off the pitch.

Highlights from the book include:

- New, inspiring and effective ways of warm-up for training.
- Warm-up programs before matches.
- Warm-up programs to improve performance at the start of the second half.

Warm-up in Football is critical reading for all who have an interest in the coaching and physiology of football.

Jens Bangsbo, PhD, Dr. Scient, has published more than 300 scientific articles and numerous book reviews and chapters and has written more than 25 books in the field of exercise physiology and football, most of which have been translated to more than ten languages. He is a former professional football player with more than 300 matches in the top league in Denmark and has played on the national team both as a youth and senior player. He has coached at the highest international level in football for Juventus FC, AEK Athens and the Danish national football team, and is currently coach of the Italian club Atalanta. He is a UEFA pro-license coach, FIFA, UEFA and AFC instructor.

Casper Skovgaard, PhD, has written a number of scientific articles and has worked as a football coach and fitness coach for a number of years. Casper is currently running the company SoccerFitness, which he started with Jens Bangsbo in 2018.

WARM-UP IN FOOTBALL

Optimize Performance and Avoid Injuries

Jens Bangsbo and Casper Skovgaard

NEW YORK AND LONDON

First published 2021
by Routledge
52 Vanderbilt Avenue, New York, NY 10017

and by Routledge
2 Park Square, Milton Park, Abingdon, Oxon, OX14 4RN

Routledge is an imprint of the Taylor & Francis Group, an informa business

© 2021 Taylor & Francis

The right of Jens Bangsbo and Casper Skovgaard to be identified as authors of this work has been asserted by them in accordance with sections 77 and 78 of the Copyright, Designs and Patents Act 1988.

All rights reserved. No part of this book may be reprinted or reproduced or utilised in any form or by any electronic, mechanical, or other means, now known or hereafter invented, including photocopying and recording, or in any information storage or retrieval system, without permission in writing from the publishers.

Trademark notice: Product or corporate names may be trademarks or registered trademarks, and are used only for identification and explanation without intent to infringe.

Library of Congress Cataloging-in-Publication Data
Names: Bangsbo, Jens, author. | Skovgaard, Casper, author.
Title: Warm-up in football : optimize performance and avoid injuries / Jens
　Bangsbo and Casper Skovgaard.
Description: New York, NY : Routledge, 2020. | Includes bibliographical
　references and index.
Identifiers: LCCN 2020053443 (print) | LCCN 2020053444 (ebook) |
　ISBN 9780367675066 (hardback) | ISBN 9780367675059 (paperback) |
　ISBN 9781003131571 (ebook)
Subjects: LCSH: Soccer—Training. | Soccer—Physiological aspects. | Exercise.
Classification: LCC GV943.9.T7 B34 2020 (print) | LCC GV943.9.T7 (ebook) |
　DDC 796.334—dc23
LC record available at https://lccn.loc.gov/2020053443
LC ebook record available at https://lccn.loc.gov/2020053444

ISBN: 978-0-367-67506-6 (hbk)
ISBN: 978-0-367-67505-9 (pbk)
ISBN: 978-1-003-13157-1 (ebk)

Typeset in ApexBembo
by Apex CoVantage, LLC

CONTENTS

List of Figures	*vii*
Preface	*ix*
Introduction	1

PART I
Characteristics of Warm-Up   3

1	Effect of Warm-Up	5
2	Principles of Warm-Up	10
3	Warm-Up of Female Players	14
4	Warm-Up of Youth Players	33

PART II
Warm-Up for Training and Testing   39

5	Preparation for Training	41
6	Warm-Up Without the Ball	53
7	Warm-Up With the Ball	83
8	Warm-Up Games	106
9	Warm-Up for Speed and Power Training	115

10 Warm-Up for Testing   138

PART III
Match Preparation   **143**

11 Warm-Up for Match   145

12 Re-warm-Up at Halftime and
    Before Extra Time   164

13 Warm-Up of Substitutes   170

Index   *201*

FIGURES

1.1	Changes in muscle and body temperature during 50 minutes of exercise.	6
1.2	The relationship between muscle temperature and sprint performance.	6
1.3	Countermovement jump height after no warm-up, normal football warm-up, 5RM warm-up and small-sided game warm-up. Note that it was only the small-sided game warm-up that improved performance	7
1.4	Agility after no warm-up, normal football warm-up, 5RM warm-up and small-sided game warm-up.	7
1.5	Blood lactate after no warm-up, normal football warm-up, 5RM warm-up and small-sided game warm-up.	8
2.1	Heart rate during a warm-up program for training and match consisting of three phases separated by two periods with dynamic stretches.	11
2.2	Major muscles of the body.	12
2.3	Different types of muscle contractions.	13
3.1	Complex	23
3.2	Center circle	24
4.1	Hit the cone	34
4.2	Hit the ball	35
4.3	Circuit	36
4.4	Technical	37
6.1	Activities and running	54
7.1	Pairs	84
7.2	Collaboration	86
7.3	Couples	87
7.4a	The line: activities and jogging	89
7.4b	The line: receive and pass	89
7.4c	The line: one-two	90
7.4d	The line: long pass and intense run with ball	91
7.5a	The square: activities and jogging	92
7.5b	The square: dribbling	93

7.5c	The square: receive and pass	93
7.5d	The square: one-two	94
7.5e	The square: diagonal	95
7.6a	The triangle: activities and jogging	96
7.6b	The triangle: dribbling	96
7.6c	The triangle: receive and pass	97
7.6d	The triangle: one-two	98
7.6e	The triangle: diagonal	98
7.7a	The Y: one touch	100
7.7b	The Y: turning	101
7.7c	The Y: one-two	102
7.8a	The cross: activities and jogging	103
7.8b	The cross: tiki-taka	104
7.8c	The cross: one-two	104
7.8d	The cross: between	105
8.1a	Phase one: 4 vs. 2	107
8.1b	Phase two: 3 vs. 3	108
8.1c	Phase three: 6 vs. 6	109
8.2	Catch	110
8.3	Heading ball	111
8.4	Touch football	112
8.5	Three colors	114
11.1	Activities and running during team warm-up for match	146
11.2	A passing drill for the whole team.	156
11.3	Core temperature and time to complete a repeated sprint test for players wearing a Blizzard survival jacket or not during a 15-minute recovery phase after a warm-up	160
12.1	High-intensity running during various periods of a match.	165
12.2	Muscle temperature before and during a match.	165
12.3	Sprint performance (average of three 30-meter sprints separated by 30 seconds of recovery) before a match, at the end of the first half, at the start of the second half and at the end of the match with or without a re-warm-up program at halftime.	166
12.4	Countermovement jump performance before a match, at the end of first half and at the start of the second half with or without a re-warm-up program at halftime consisting of 7 minutes of running and activities	166
12.5	Body and muscle temperature before a match, at the end of the first half and the start of the second half with or without a re-warm-up program at halftime consisting of 7 minutes of running and activities	167
12.6	Heart rate response during the first 3 minutes at the start of the second half with or without a re-warm-up program at halftime consisting of 7 minutes of running and activities which ended 1 minute before the start of the second half.	168
13.1	Mean moderate, high-speed and sprint running distance of substitutes and players performing the entire match at the same time during the match.	171
13.2	Mean moderate, high-speed and sprint running distance of substitutes and when the same players started the match (divided into first and second halves).	171
13.3	Activities and running	177

PREFACE

Warm-up is boring. Many football players would prefer not to warm up, but they have understood the values. Warm-up should rather be called "preparation activities," as the exercises are to make sure that the players can perform during the following training or match with a minimal risk of getting injured. Often the coach spends too much time on the warm-up and makes it too intense. For example, there is no point in doing an intense warm-up finishing with several sprints if the players subsequently are doing a tactical session, where they are standing for a significant part of the training. Thus, the warm-up has to be adjusted to the purpose by choosing the right exercises and drills.

Through a long life in football, we have experienced many inefficient warm-up sessions. Sometimes warm-up and football training sessions may be boring in order to achieve the goal. However, carefully considering the content of the warm-up not only serves the purpose of stimulating and preparing the players, but it should also be useful for the players' development. Often the warm-up lasts 20 minutes, which covers a significant part of a training session with a duration of 60–90 minutes, so elements (e.g., agility and technical) of value for the players' development should be incorporated.

In this book, we provide a basic understanding of the value of warming up and present a significant number of warm-up programs for training and matches to be used in various conditions, whether you are training professional, amateur or youth players.

Warm-up has to be motivating and efficient!

Jens Bangsbo and Casper Skovgaard

INTRODUCTION

Every training session and match should begin with a warm-up in order to improve performance and reduce the risk of injuries. In addition to physical effects, the warm-up also has psychological benefits. Before a match, it may help some players to control their anxiety and focus on their tasks during the match. For training, a warm-up can stimulate the players and prepare them mentally for the following exercises.

This book provides the scientific evidence for the effect of warming up and describes how performance is closely related to the muscle temperature elevated by warm-up. Furthermore, the book explains how warm-up before a match and the second half does improve the outcome in football.

A large number of warm-up programs for training both with and without the ball are presented, with specifications of the technical and tactical elements being trained. The warm-up phase is a preparation for the following training and should ensure that the players can conduct the training with an optimal outcome. Therefore, for each program it is specified which type of training, such as tactical, technical, speed and power training, the program is aimed for. Warm-up games are also provided. These can be used to stimulate the players and to make sure that all muscles for football are activated and warmed up properly. At the same time, players also develop technical and tactical elements as described for each warm-up game. Specific programs for female and youth players are also provided.

Most coaches and players have a specific way of doing the warm-up for matches. Often the warm-up is based on tradition, and in many cases the players are doing too much and are working too hard. The players may believe it is necessary in order to perform optimally in the match, but an intense warm-up may have a negative effect on performance, either because they are fatigued when the match starts or they will be tired toward the end of the match due to spending too much of their energy stores during the warm-up. Warm-up programs for matches are provided. They also address the inherent challenges that professional players often have in finishing the warm-up 15–20 minutes before the start of a match.

Warm-up at halftime is not often practiced, but it does benefit the players. Performance at the start of the second half is actually lowered if the players do not get the muscle temperature back to the same level as before halftime. These issues are addressed in Chapter 12, where practical suggestions are also provided. A specific focus is also on the warm-up of substitutes in order to ensure they perform optimally when they are entering the match.

In order to conduct a valid fitness test, it is of great importance that the warm-up is standardized and specific for the test. In Chapter 10, appropriate warm-up programs for various tests used in football are presented.

With the precise guidelines provided in the book, there is no excuse for not doing a proper warm-up—whether it is for training, matches, or at halftime or for the substitutes—benefiting the players.

PART I
Characteristics of Warm-Up

As the term "warm-up" indicates, the exercises performed before an activity, such as training or a match, does lead to increased body and muscle temperature, which will improve performance. Warm-up programs also have other beneficial effects and should follow certain principles to be efficient, as described in the following chapters, where programs for youth and female players are also provided.

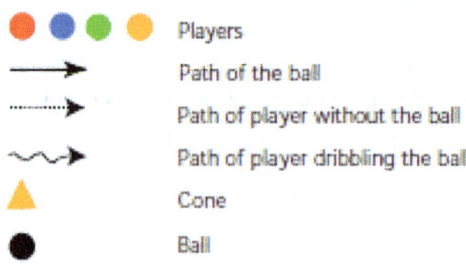

1

EFFECT OF WARM-UP

This chapter describes the effect of warm-up with a focus on muscle and body temperature as well as performance. In addition, the effect of warm-up is also to avoid injuries, and the value of using stretching exercise during the warm-up is discussed.

Warm-up Increases Muscle and Body Temperature

During exercise, the active muscles produce heat. As the intensity of the exercise increases, more heat is generated. Some of the heat is transferred from the muscles into the blood and is dispersed throughout the body. Thus, exercising with large muscle groups not only causes an increase in muscle temperature but also results in a considerable rise in body temperature. During intense exercise, muscle temperature may rise to 43°C, while body temperature can reach 41°C. Figure 1.1 illustrates what happens to the temperature of muscle and body during 50 minutes with exercise at constant moderate intensity. The muscle temperature reaches a stable level after about 10 minutes, whereas the body temperature is still rising after 50 minutes.

Warm-up Increases Performance

A rise in muscle temperature increases the ability of the muscles to produce energy during exercise. This is one reason for the improvement in performance observed after a warm-up. Figure 1.2 shows the relationship between muscle temperature and performance on a cycle ergometer during a brief sprint. From the results presented in Figures 1.1 and 1.2, it can be concluded that a warm-up should last for at least 10 minutes for the players to fully benefit from the increase in muscle temperature.

The type of warm-up in football also affects performance. A study of male football players investigated the effect of three different types of warm-up:

1. 3 repetitions of a small-sided game (3 vs. 3) with 2 minutes of play separated by a 2-minute recovery period; thus, a total duration of 10 minutes. The size of the pitch was increased from 20 m × 12 m in the first repetition to 25 m × 15 m in the second repetition and 30 m × 18 m in the third repetition.
2. 5 minutes of jogging, followed by a 5-repetition maximum (RM) seated leg press.

6 Characteristics of Warm-Up

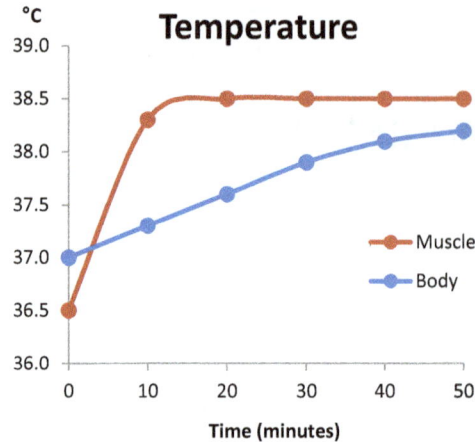

FIGURE 1.1 Changes in muscle (red) and body (blue) temperature during 50 minutes of exercise. The body temperature increases gradually, whereas the muscle temperature increases only during the first 10 minutes and then remains constant.

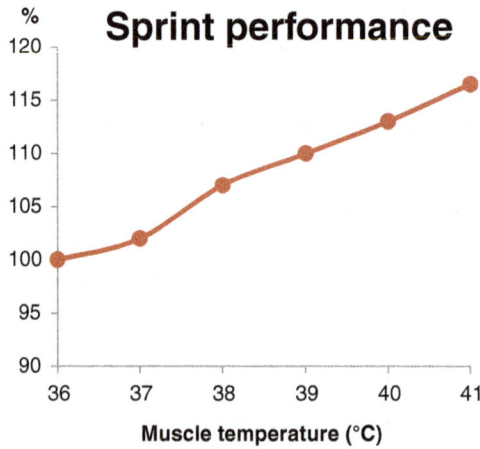

FIGURE 1.2 The relationship between muscle temperature and sprint performance. Note that the higher the muscle temperature, the better the performance (e.g., at a muscle temperature of 41°C, performance was 15% greater than a muscle temperature of 37°C).

3. A "normal warm-up" routine in football lasting approximately 23 minutes, which included general activities, such as butt-kicks, high-knees and air squats, performed at medium intensity for 6 minutes, followed by specific movements (i.e., back and forth sprinting and change of direction) performed at high intensity for 9 minutes. The last part was ball-control activities, such as passing, dribbling and run-throughs, performed at high intensity for 6 minutes.

4 minutes after the warm-up, the players performed various tests and physiological measurements were carried out. Countermovement jump height improved following the small-sided game (6%) and slightly with the leg-press warm-up (2%), but not after the "normal warm-up" (see Figure 1.3). Similarly, agility improved only after the small-sided game (4%) and leg-press warm-up (5%; Figure 1.4). Mean 20-meter sprint time improved following the leg-press warm-up when

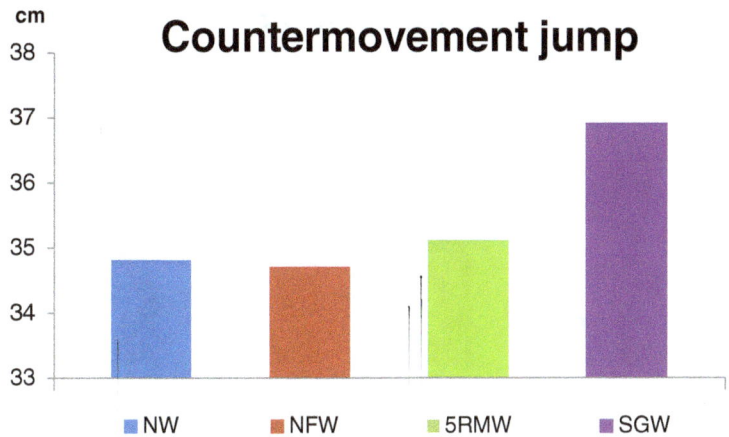

FIGURE 1.3 Countermovement jump height after no warm-up (NW), normal football warm-up (NFW), 5RM warm-up (5RMW) and small-sided game warm-up (SGW). Note that it was only the small-sided game warm-up that improved performance.

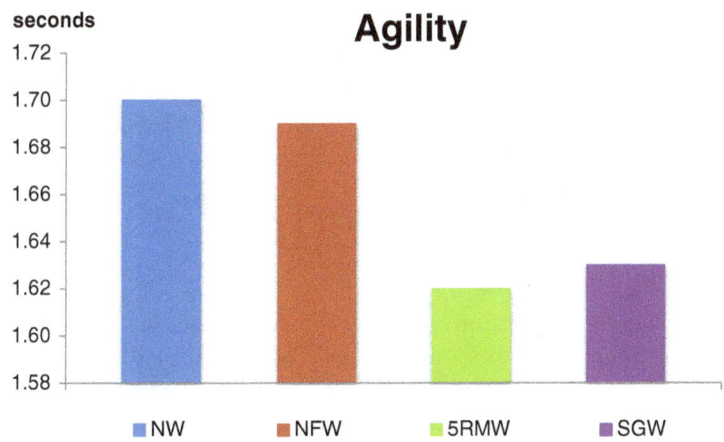

FIGURE 1.4 Agility after no warm-up (NW), normal football warm-up (NFW), 5RM warm-up (5RMW) and small-sided game warm-up (SGW). Note that both the small-sided game warm-up and 5RM warm-up improved performance (lower time to complete the task), whereas the normal football warm-up had no effect.

compared to the small-sided game (9% more) and "normal warm-up" routine (7% more). Blood lactate was highest following the small-sided game and "normal warm-up" (see Figure 1.5). Apparently, leg-press and small-sided game warm-up were more effective than a traditional 23-minute warm-up protocol in improving performance. It may be that the "normal warm-up" negatively affected the players' performance due to development of fatigue.

Thus, it can be concluded that a warm-up of rather short duration can improve performance, and too much high-intensity exercise during warm-up, as in normal football warm-up, may eliminate the positive effect of warm-up.

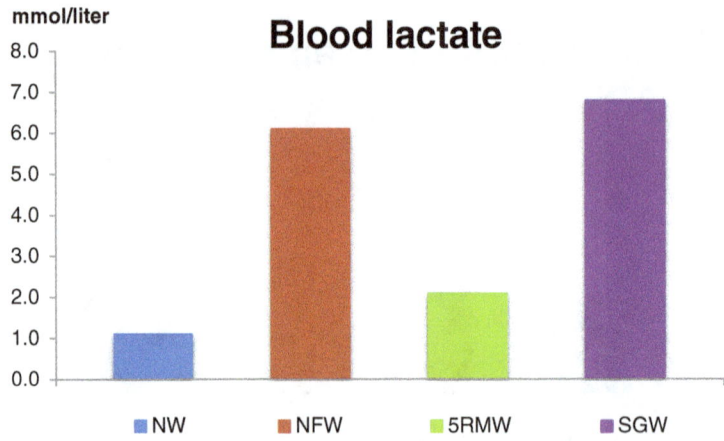

FIGURE 1.5 Blood lactate after no warm-up (NW), normal football warm-up (NFW), 5RM warm-up (5RMW) and small-sided game warm-up (SGW). Note that the small-sided game warm-up and normal football warm-up increased blood lactate significantly.

Warm-up Reduces the Risk of Injuries

Many injuries occur due to an insufficient warm-up. A cold muscle is relatively rigid and resistant to sudden increases in tension caused by rapid movements. When the elastic components of the muscle are unable to accommodate the external tensions, the muscle will rupture. This is commonly referred to as a "pulled" muscle. Thus, by warming up the muscles and tendons, the risk of injuries is significantly reduced.

Stretching During Warm-up

The value of stretching during a warm-up has been discussed for many years. Previously it was believed that static stretching (i.e., the position is held for more than 10 seconds) improved performance, but there is evidence that the opposite is the case. Thus, a bout of static stretching has been shown to lead to significant reductions in maximum muscle strength and power. On the other hand, dynamic stretching (i.e., moving while stretching) has positive effects on subsequent performance, such as on force, power, sprint and jump performance. It also increases the range of motion around a joint, which reduces stiffness of the muscle-tendon unit. Nonetheless, the increase in muscular performance is not just related to the improved range of motion but also to the increase in muscle temperature associated with dynamic stretching.

It should be emphasized that some studies have shown no effect of stretching. Thus, the effects of static (5 or 30 seconds, 5 repetitions per muscle group), dynamic (seven lower body and two upper body muscles) and no stretches, performed as part of a comprehensive warm-up program, were examined in team sport athletes. Participants felt they were more likely to perform well when stretching was performed as part of the warm-up, irrespective of stretch type. However, no effect of muscle stretching was observed on flexibility, sprint running, jumping and change of direction compared to no stretching. Thus, this study showed that the inclusion of short durations of either static or dynamic stretching did not affect performance when conducted as part of a comprehensive warm-up program.

Despite the different results from scientific studies, the players may benefit from dynamic stretching to increase range of motion and to enhance sprint, jump, muscle force and power performance. It has been shown that it is better to use controlled dynamic stretching, rather than ballistic stretching (i.e., dynamic stretching with high velocities).

Summary

Warm-up does increase body and muscle temperature, leading to elevated performance and reduced risk of getting injured. If the warm-up is too intense, however, the positive effects of warm-up may be abolished. Static stretching longer than 5 seconds should be avoided during the warm-up, as it has been shown to reduce performance. On the other hand, dynamic stretching may increase performance and should be part of the warm-up.

Bibliography

Blazevich AJ, Gill ND, Kvorning T, Kay AD, Goh A, Hilton B, Drinkwater EJ, Behm DG. No effect of muscle stretching within a full, dynamic warm-up on athletic performance. *Medicine & Science in Sports & Exercise* 50: 1258–1266, 2018.

Kendall BJ. The acute effects of static stretching compared to dynamic stretching with and without an active warm up on anaerobic performance. *International Journal of Exercise Science* 10, 1: 53–61, 2017.

Opplert J, Babault N. Acute effects of dynamic stretching on muscle flexibility and performance: an analysis of the current literature. *Sports Medicine* 48: 299–325, 2018.

Walsh GS. Effect of static and dynamic muscle stretching as part of warm up procedures on knee joint proprioception and strength. *Human Movement Science* 55: 189–195, 2017.

Van den Tillaar R, von Heimburg E. Comparison of two types of warm-up upon repeated-sprint performance in experienced soccer players. *The Journal of Strength & Conditioning Research* 30: 2258–2265, 2016.

Zois J, Bishop DJ, Ball K, Aughey RJ. High-intensity warm-ups elicit superior performance to a current soccer warm-up routine. *Journal of Science and Medicine in Sport* 14: 522–528, 2011.

2
PRINCIPLES OF WARM-UP

Some essential components of warm-up are described in this chapter.

Gradually Increase in Intensity

The exercise intensity should be low at the beginning of a warm-up and gradually increase in order to avoid the players getting overloaded and injured. When warming up with the ball, the tasks should be technically easy to perform. Otherwise, there is a risk that the overall activity level will be too low, and the warm-up will not have the desired effect. A warm-up program should also include dynamic stretching exercises, and when using static stretching, the position should be held for a maximum of 5 seconds.

The warm-up should be initiated with some exercises that activate large muscle groups, for example, jogging with or without a ball. After approximately 5 minutes of activities and whole body exercise, light dynamic stretching can be performed. The warm-up should then be continued with exercises for the main muscle groups used during football, which can be achieved by doing drills with the ball (see Chapter 7). After another series of dynamic stretching, the intensity of the warm-up activities can be increased and should be high toward the end of a warm-up performed before a speed endurance training session or match. However, this may not be necessary when warming up for other types of training, such as tactical training, since the coach and the players can control the exercise intensity of the subsequent training drills. An example of the fluctuation in heart rate of a player during a warm-up program before a speed training session is shown in Figure 2.1.

Duration

The effect of duration of warm-up for male football players has also been investigated. In a study, a 10-minute warm-up program was compared to a 20-minute warm-up program for an elite football team. The 10-minute warm-up consisted of 8 ×50-meter runs with increasing speed reaching about 95% of maximum. Each run was separated by 1 minute of recovery, where the players performed dynamic stretches for the shoulder, hip, knee and ankle joints. After the last 50 m run, 3 minutes of active recovery was taken before the start of a repeated-sprint test.

The 20-minute warm-up started with 5 minutes of the Yo-Yo Intermittent Recovery level 1 test. Then, subjects walked for 2 minutes at 5.5 km/h on a treadmill, followed by 5 minutes of

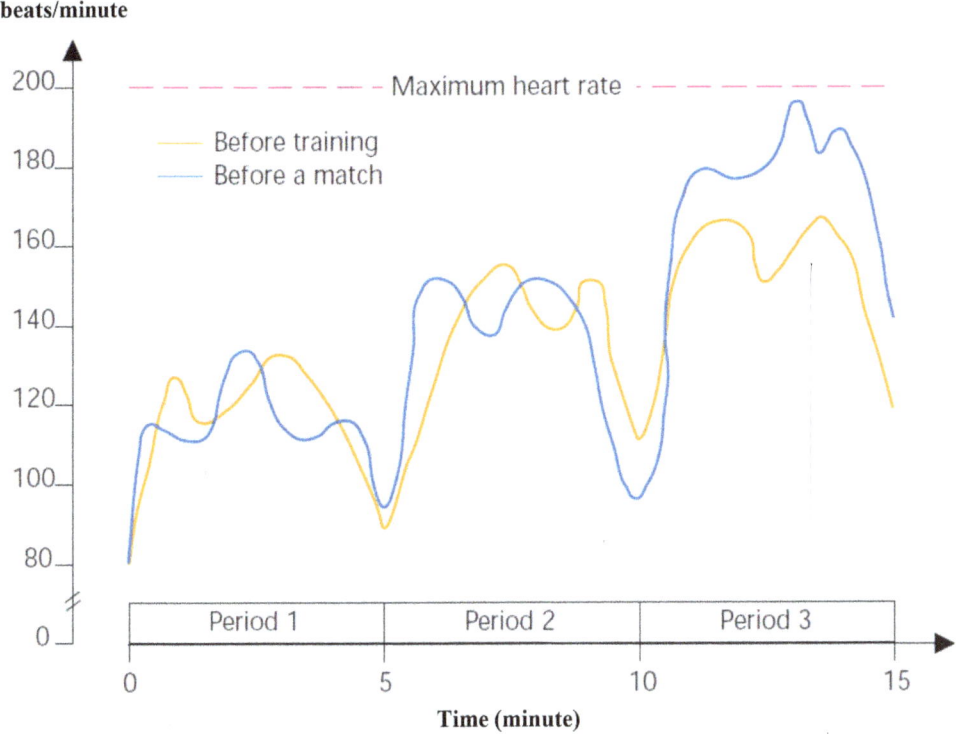

FIGURE 2.1 Heart rate during a warm-up program for training and match consisting of three phases separated by two periods with dynamic stretches.

running at 9 km/h. After this, dynamic stretches were performed for 4 minutes, and then running on a treadmill at 12 km/h for 2 minutes was followed by 1 minute of running at 15 km/h. Finally, subjects performed 4 runs of 30 m at 80%, 85%, 90% and 95% of self-estimated maximum 30 m speed. After 3 minutes of active recovery, the repeated-sprint test was conducted.

In the test, the players performed 8 × 30-meter sprints separated by 30 seconds of rest, and no difference in performance between the two programs was observed. Thus, the 10-minute warm-up was as effective as the 20-minute warm-up, and as the players felt the 20-minute warm-up was more demanding, it is recommended to keep the warm-up shorter than 15 minutes unless there are other purposes of the warm-up, such as developing technical skills.

Importance of Environment Temperature

Both weather and temperature must be considered when planning a warm-up. When the air temperature is high, the temperature of the muscles and body increases more rapidly than in a cold environment, and less time for warm-up is needed. Nevertheless, it is important to warm up in order to specifically increase the temperature of the muscles. In a study at an environmental temperature of 33°C, female football players completed a 15-minute warm-up program consisting of jogging, skipping by moving the legs in various directions, and sprinting alternated with jogging. The warm-up increased the core temperature by approximately 1°C and improved 40-meter sprint time by 3% (5.52 vs. 5.66 seconds).

12 Characteristics of Warm-Up

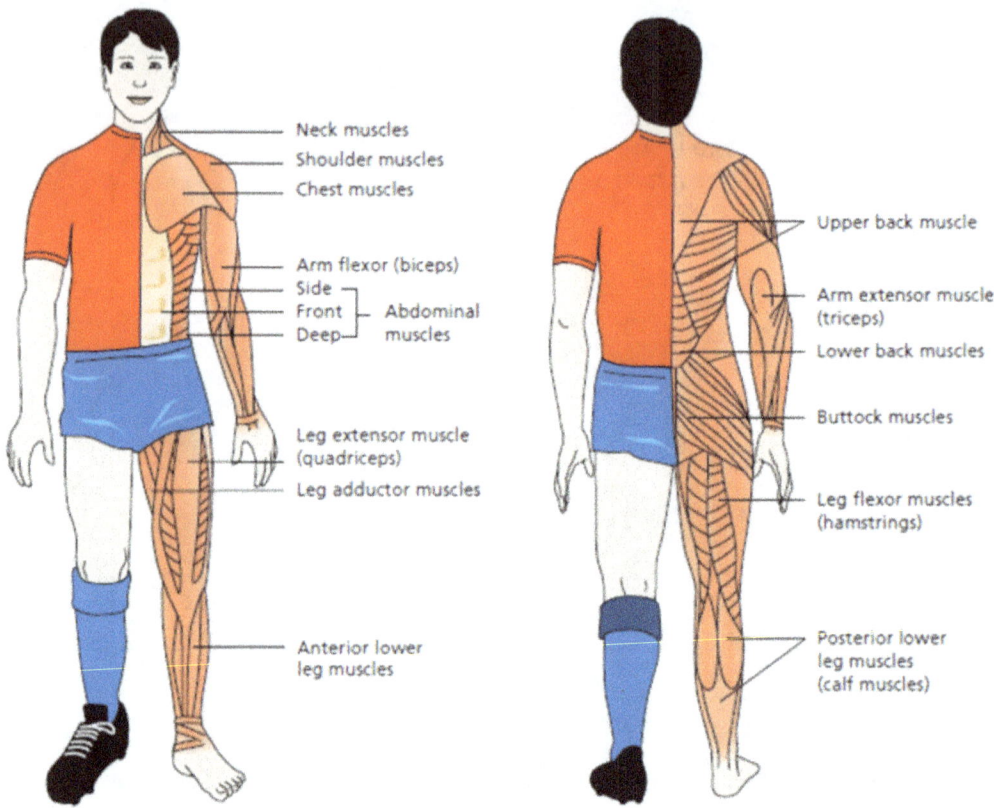

FIGURE 2.2 Major muscles of the body.

In cold weather, it is advisable that players wear extra clothes and perhaps a beanie to decrease the loss of heat from the body and head, and to enable the muscle and body temperature to increase more rapidly.

Muscles of the Body and Characterization of Movements

In order to understand the value and effect of the different exercises presented in the book, it is important to know the muscles in the body as illustrated in Figure 2.2, and how the muscles can contract in different ways. Skeletal muscles can contract in three different ways (see Figure 2.3):

- Concentric contraction, where the muscle produces force while being shortened.
- Eccentric contraction, where the muscle produces force while being lengthened.
- Isometric contraction, where the muscle develops force with no visible movement of the joint.

Summary

In order to optimize the warm-up program for a training session or match, it is important to understand the basic components of warm-up as provided in this chapter. The intensity during a warm-up should be gradually increased, and for specific training sessions, such as speed training

Principles of Warm-Up **13**

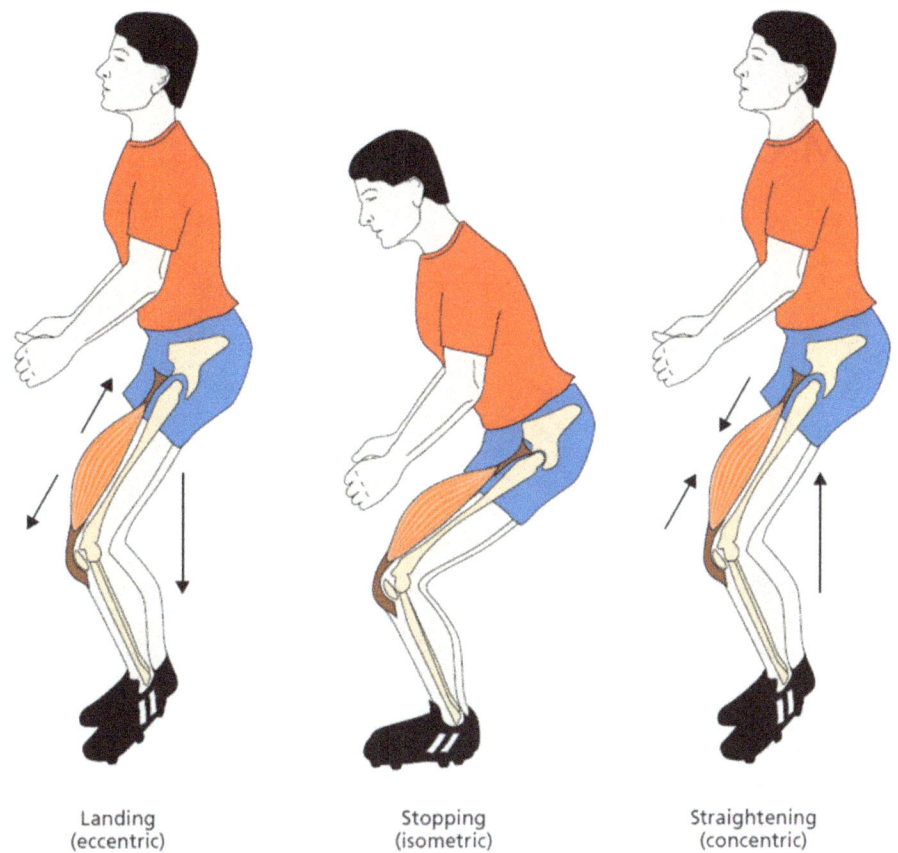

Landing (eccentric) Stopping (isometric) Straightening (concentric)

FIGURE 2.3 Different types of muscle contractions. In an eccentric contraction, the muscle lengthens (left); in an isometric contraction, the muscle length is unchanged (middle); in a concentric contraction, the muscle shortens (right).

and match, the intensity should be at maximum toward the end of the warm-up. It is sufficient to perform 10 minutes of warm-up to get the performance benefits. In a hot environment, it is also necessary to warm up, but it should be less intense than during normal conditions.

Bibliography

Bangsbo J. *Aerobic and anaerobic training in soccer.* www.soccerfitness.expert, 2012.
Bangsbo J, Andersen J. *Power training in football.* www.soccerfitness.expert, 2015.
Bangsbo J, Peitersen B. *Soccer systems and strategies.* Human Kinetics, 2000.
Somboonwong J, Chutimakul L, Sanguanrungsirikul S. Core temperature changes and sprint performance of elite female soccer players after a 15-minute warm-up in a hot-humid environment. *The Journal of Strength & Conditioning Research* 29: 262–269, 2015.
Van den Tillaar R, von Heimburg E. Comparison of two types of warm-up upon repeated-sprint performance in experienced soccer players. *The Journal of Strength & Conditioning Research* 30: 2258–2265, 2016.

3

WARM-UP OF FEMALE PLAYERS

There is no difference between female and male players in the response to warm up. However, the risk of a severe injury, such as damage to the anterior cruciate ligament (ACL) during training and match play, is three to five times higher for female than male football players. Based on this knowledge, the effect of a comprehensive warm-up program designed to improve strength, awareness and neuromuscular control was investigated in 2,000 female players aged 13–17 years from 125 football clubs in Norway. The female players were followed for one season, and the program reduced the risk of injury by one-third and the risk of a severe injury was halved. The warm-up program used in the study is presented in this chapter (see Program 1).

In addition to the overall increased risk of a severe knee injury in female players, studies suggest that women are more vulnerable to anterior cruciate ligament injuries during the ovulatory phase of the menstrual cycle; this is due to the effect of hormonal fluctuations on the laxity of ligaments. It is therefore recommended to conduct a warm-up program that include specific exercises for activation of hamstrings, quadriceps, glutes, and hip and core muscles. Proper positioning of the feet, knees and hips should be emphasized during the execution of the exercises, as well as proper movements for jumping and landing (e.g., knees must not move inwards). Given next are two warm-up programs that are useful for female players.

Program 1: Complex

This program lasts 20 minutes and consists of running at low speed, dynamic stretches and activities including controlled contacts with a partner. The course is 30 meters long with 6 pairs of parallel cones about 5 meters apart (see Figure 3.1). The players are organized in two rows and conduct the exercises in pairs. The players perform the exercise twice on the way out, and they run at moderate speed back to the starting position.

0–7 Minutes: Running and Activities

This part focuses on running and activities that will increase the heart rate while also activating leg and hip muscles. Coordination and balance are also challenged.

Warm-Up of Female Players **15**

1. *Running*: Run to the last pair of cones. 2 repetitions.

2. *Hip out*: Pull the knee toward the chest and move it to the side as far as possible; lower the leg, working the opposite abductor. 2 repetitions.

3. *Hip in*: Pull the knee out and up, then move it in while still in the air; lower the leg, working the opposite leg adductor. 2 repetitions.

4. *Circling*: Run forward to the first set of cones, and then shuffle sideways to meet the partner in the middle of the two cones. Shuffle in a circle around the partner and then return to the row of cones. Repeat for each pair of cones. 2 repetitions.

16 Characteristics of Warm-Up

5. *Jumping with shoulder contact*: Run forward to the first pair of cones. Shuffle sideways to meet the partner in the middle and then jump sideways toward the partner to make shoulder-to-shoulder contact. Land on both feet with the hips and knees bent. Do not let the knees move inwards. 2 repetitions.

6. *Quick run*: Run quickly to the second set of cones and then backpedal quickly to the first pair of cones. Repeat the drill by running two cones forward and one cone backward. 2 repetitions.

7–17 Minutes: Strength, Jumps and Balance

This part focuses on strength, jumps and balance and consists of six exercises (each with three levels of difficulty).

7. *The plank*: Lying face down, support the body on forearms and feet with elbows directly under the shoulders. For all levels, the body should be in a straight line with tension on the abdominal and gluteal muscles, and the back should not sway or arch.

   - *Level 1—on both legs*: Hold the position. 3 × 20–30 seconds.

   - *Level 2—alternate legs*: Lift each leg in turn, hold for 2 seconds. 3 × 20–30 seconds.

   - *Level 3—one leg lift*: Lift one leg about 10–15 cm off the ground and hold the position for 20–30 seconds. Do not let the opposite hip dip down. Take a short break, change legs and repeat. 3 × 20–30 seconds on each leg.

18 Characteristics of Warm-Up

8. *Side plank*: Lean on the forearm and the side of the foot with the body in a straight line from shoulder to foot. The elbow of the supporting arm should be directly beneath the shoulder.

    - *Level 1—static*: Shoulders, hips and knees are in a straight line. 3 × 20–30 seconds (each side).

    - *Level 2—dynamic*: Continuously lower the hip to the ground and raise it back up. 3 × 20–30 seconds (each side).

    - *Level 3—with leg lift*: Continuously lift and lower the upper leg. 3 × 20–30 seconds (each side).

9. *Nordic hamstring*: Kneeling on a soft surface, a partner holds below the calves to keep the lower legs down. The body should be straight from the shoulders to the knees throughout the exercise. Lean forward as far as possible while controlling the movement with the hamstrings and gluteal muscles. When the position can no longer be held, take the weight of the fall with the hands.

    - *Level 1*: 3–5 repetitions.
    - *Level 2*: 7–10 repetitions.

- *Level 3*: 12–15 repetitions.

10. *Single leg balance*: Standing on one leg.

- *Level 1—holding ball*: Balance on one leg while holding a ball with both hands. The exercise can be made more difficult by standing on the toes. 2 × 30 seconds (each leg).

- *Level 2—throwing ball with partner*: Throw the ball to one another. 2 × 30 seconds (each leg).

- *Level 3—testing partner*: In turns, try to keep balance while trying to push the partner off-balance in different directions. 2 × 30 seconds (each leg).

20 Characteristics of Warm-Up

11. *Squat*: Stand with feet hip-width apart and hands on the hips.

    - *Level 1—with toe raise*: Perform a squat by bending hips and knees to 90 degrees. When legs are straight, stand on the toes and then slowly lower down into a squat again. 2 × 30 seconds.

    - *Level 2—walking lunges*: Similar to forward lunging; bend the leading leg until hip and knee are flexed to 90 degrees. 2 × 30 seconds.

    - *Level 3—one leg squat*: Stand on one leg, loosely holding onto something or someone. Slowly bend the knee as far as possible. 2 × 10 repetitions (each leg).

12. *Jumping*: Different type of jumps with controlled landing.

    - *Level 1—vertical jumps*: Bend the legs until the knees are flexed to 90 degrees, and hold for 2 seconds. From the squat position, jump as high as possible. Land softly with hips and knees slightly bent. 2 × 30 seconds.

    - *Level 2—lateral jumps*: Jump approximately 1 meter sideways onto one leg. Land gently and maintain balance with each jump. 2 × 30 seconds.

22 Characteristics of Warm-Up

- *Level 3—star jumps*: On one leg, jump forward, backward, from side to side, and diagonally to create a star pattern in the surface. 2 × 30 seconds.

17–20 Minutes: Running

This part consists of running at high speed with football-specific movements, including sudden changes in direction. The exercises are performed from one side of the pitch to the other, while jogging is performed on the way back.

13. *Fast running*: Run across the pitch at 75%–85% of maximum pace. 2 repetitions.

14. *Bounding run*: Run with high bounding steps by doing a high-knee lift and an exaggerated arm swing for each step (opposite arm and leg). 2 repetitions.

Warm-Up of Female Players **23**

15. *Change of direction run*: Jog 4–5 steps, then plant on the outside leg and cut to change direction. Accelerate and sprint 5–7 steps at high speed (80%–90% maximum pace) before decelerating and a new plant and cut. 2 repetitions.

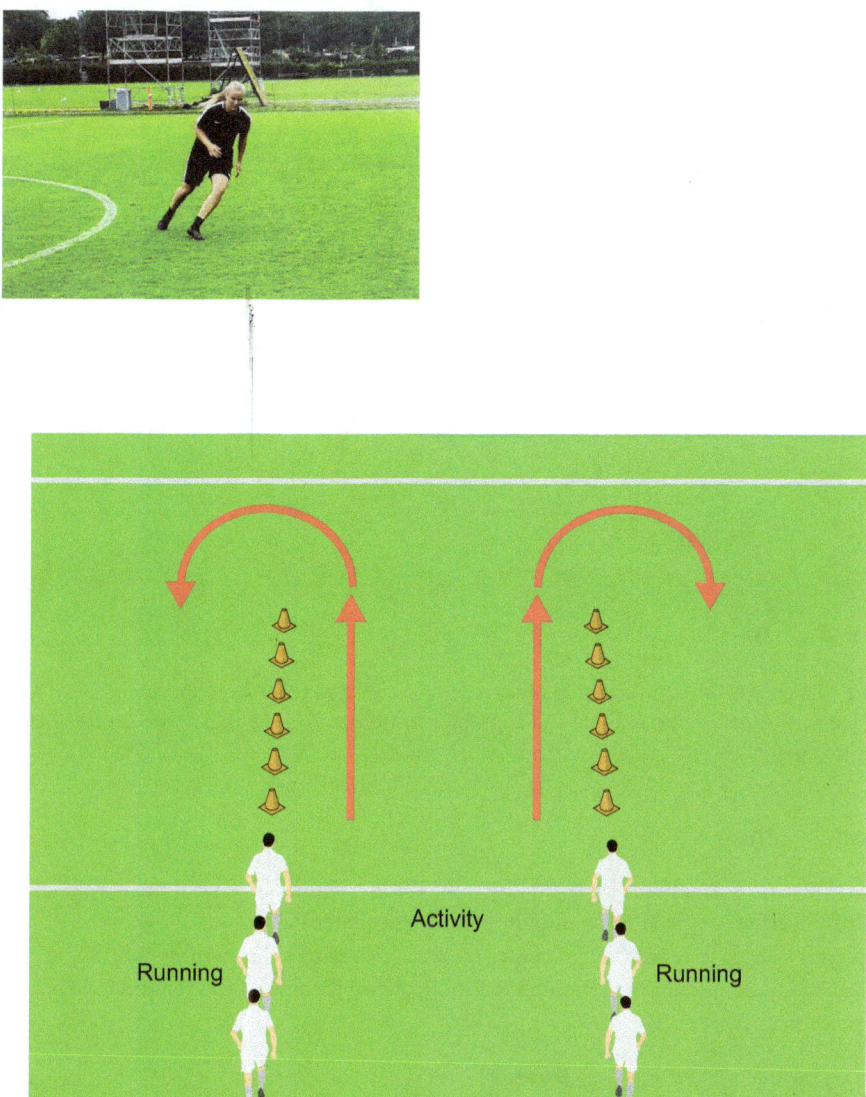

FIGURE 3.1 The course is 30 meters long with 6 pairs of parallel cones about 5 meters apart. The players are organized in two rows and are conducting the exercises in pairs. The players are performing the exercise twice on the way out, and they run at moderate speed back to the starting position.

24 Characteristics of Warm-Up

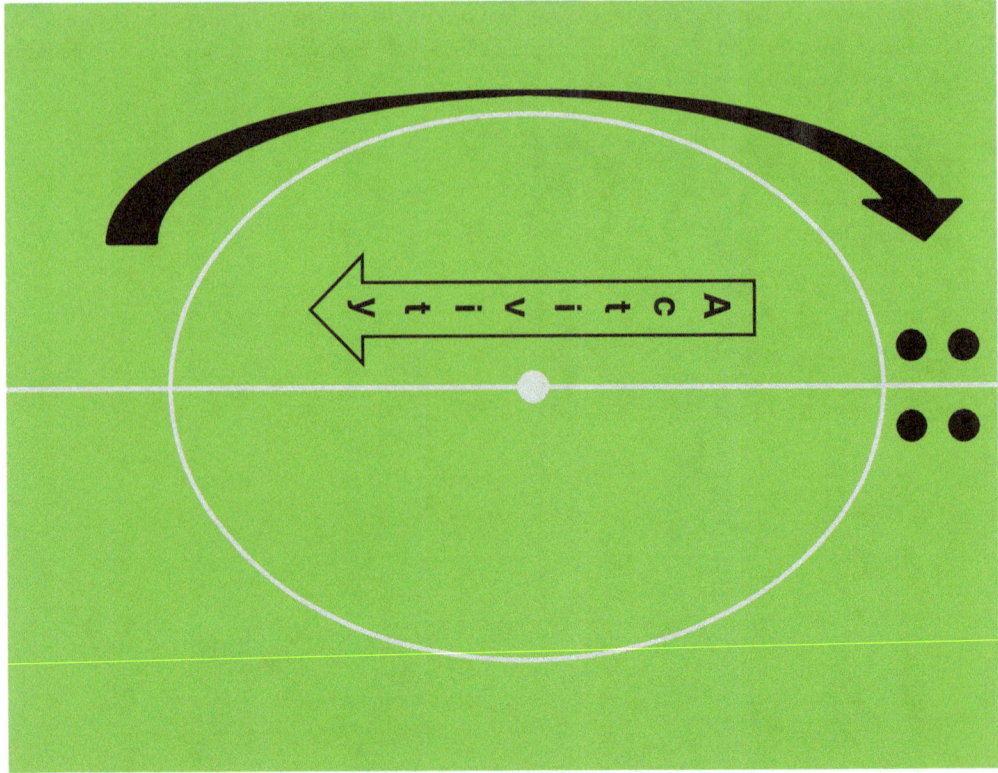

FIGURE 3.2 The players start on one side of the center circle, which marks the starting point. The activities are performed on the midline and running is conducted on the line of the center circle back to the starting point.

Program 2: Center Circle

This program lasts 15 minutes. Players are organized at the center circle with the players moving at the lines of the center circle and the midline within the center circle.

The players start on one side of the center circle, which marks the starting point. The activities are performed on the midline and running is conducted on the line of the center circle back to the starting point (see Figure 3.2).

Warm-Up of Female Players **25**

0–4 Minutes: Dynamic Stretches

1. *Hips in*: Pull the knee out and up, then move it in while still in the air; lower the leg, working the opposite leg adductor.

2. *Hips out*: Pull the knee toward the chest and move it to the side as far as possible; lower the leg, working the opposite abductor.

3. *Knee to chest*: Move the knee toward the chest; the leg kicks out and down.

26 Characteristics of Warm-Up

4. *Lateral kick*: Keeping the body and leg straight, kick to the side.

5. *Back kick*: Keeping the body and leg straight, kick the leg back and pull the opposite arm toward the back leg.

6. *Kick with a twist*: Keeping the body straight, perform a forward kick with a twist.

7. *High kick*: Keeping the body straight, perform a forward kick with a straight leg and extended foot. Clapping under the knee will increase the stretch.

4–9 Minutes: Activities

8. *Butt kicks*: Heels touch the glutes; arms move in the same way as when running.

9. *High knees*: Move the knees to horizontal (one at a time).

10. *Skips*: Pull the knee into the chest; use arms actively to contribute to each skip.

28 Characteristics of Warm-Up

11. *Lateral shuffles*: Move sideways with a low center of gravity. Change of side after 3 repetitions.

12. *Carioca*: Move sideways, alternating between crossing the back leg in front and behind the front leg.

13. *Backward running*: Run backward.

14. *Backward shuffles*: Same as "lateral shuffles," but backward; look over the shoulder to orientate.

15. *Walking forward lunge*: Lunge forward and bend the leading leg until the hip and knee are flexed to 90 degrees.

9–12 Minutes: Jumps

16. *Single leg lateral jump*: Jump approximately 1 meter and land on one leg. Then jump to the other leg. Land gently and maintain balance with each jump.

17. *Squat jump*: Squat by bending hips and knees to 90 degrees. From this position, do a jump as high as possible.

18. *Jump lunge*: Move to a forward lunge position. Jump as high as possible and switch position of the legs in the air to land with the opposite leg forward.

19. *Jump with shoulder contact and controlled landing*: Jog 4–5 steps, then coordinate a jump with shoulder-to-shoulder contact with a partner. Land on both feet with the hips and knees bent.

12–15 Minutes: Accelerations

20. *Cuts*: Jog 4–5 steps, then plant on the outside leg to cut and change direction. Accelerate and sprint 5–7 steps at high speed, decelerate, and do a new plant and cut.

21. *Go-stop-go*: Accelerate forward 5 meters, decelerate, take 2–3 quick steps backward, and then accelerate forward 5 meters.

22. *Header and go*: Jump as high as possible, land on both feet, and accelerate for 5 meters.

Summary

Female players have a higher risk of injury, especially to the knees, and female players will therefore benefit from a warm-up including specific exercises for the muscles around the knees and hips.

Bibliography

Bjordal JM, Arnly F, Hannestad B, Strand T. Epidemiology of anterior cruciate ligament injuries in soccer. *The American Journal of Sports Medicine* 25, 3: 341–345, 1997.

Herzberg SD, Motu'apuaka ML, Lambert W, Fu R, Brady J, Guise JM. The effect of menstrual cycle and contraceptives on ACL injuries and laxity: a systematic review and meta-analysis. *The Orthopaedic Journal of Sports Medicine* 5, 7: 2325967117718781, 2017.

Powell JW, Barber-Foss KD. Sex-related injury patterns among selected high school sports. *The American Journal of Sports Medicine* 28, 3: 385–391, 2000.

Soligard T, Myklebust G, Steffen K, Holme I, Silvers H, Bizzini M, Junge A, Dvorak J, Bahr R, Andersen TE. Comprehensive warm-up programme to prevent injuries in young female footballers: cluster randomised controlled trial. *British Medical Journal* 337: a2469, 2008.

4
WARM-UP OF YOUTH PLAYERS

Youth players (under 15 years) usually have greater flexibility than adult players, and thus they do not need as comprehensive a warm-up as the senior players. The warm-up phase should focus on developing the youth players' technical and agility skills. Thus, the warm-up drills should include exercises that challenge the technical ability and coordination of the players. Given next are a number of drills and a program that can be used for warming up with youth players at various ages. The duration of the drills is 10–20 minutes, and it is recommended to do 3–5 minutes of activities with the ball before playing.

Drill 1: Hit the Cone

This drill primarily develops dribbling skills of the youngest players. The player should hit as many cones as possible within 30 seconds.

Age group: 6–10 years.
Preparation for: Tactical training and technical training.
Technical elements: Dribbling and passing/shooting.
Players: 15 (10–20).
Dimension: 20 m × 30 m (see Figure 4.1).
Organization: Each player has a ball and starts at different positions.
Equipment: 15 balls and 25 cones.

Variations:

1. Only three touches before "shooting."

    - Develops the players' ability to shoot/pass.

2. Can only hit a cone that is standing.

    - Becomes more competitive.

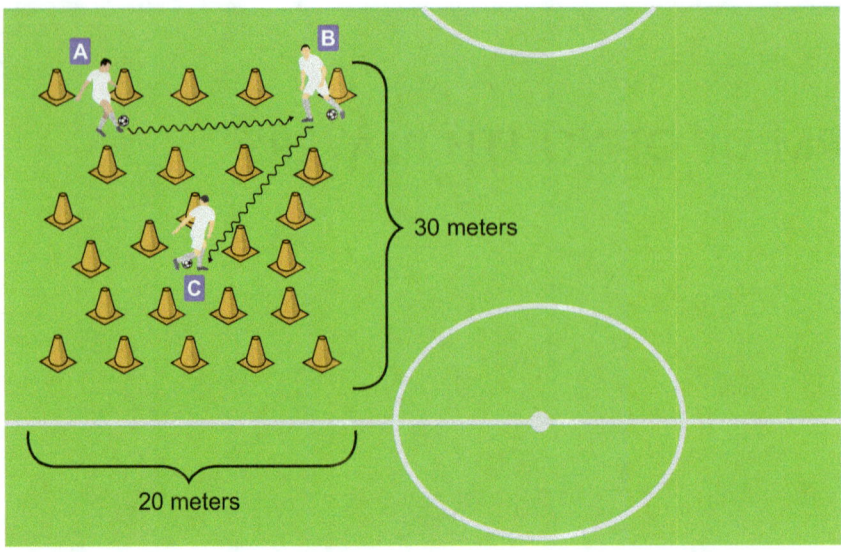

FIGURE 4.1 Hit the cone.

Hints:

- Fun activity.
- Players should be encouraged to "attack" the cones.

Drill 2: Hit the Ball

This drill mainly develops the passing skills of young players. Players should hit the ball in the middle and get the ball to the opposition zone. Players can kick the balls coming from the opposition zone, but they have to leave the balls arriving from the middle zone (they cannot kick them). The team that has the least balls (from the middle zone) after a given time (e.g., 3 minutes) wins.

Age group: 8–12 years.
Preparation for: Tactical training and technical training.
Technical elements: Passing/shooting.
Players: 20 (10–26).
Dimension: 40 m × 40 m divided into two outer zones with the middle zone being 10 meters (see Figure 4.2).
Organization: Each team is placed in one of the outer zones and has 5 balls. 10 balls are placed in the middle zone.
Equipment: 20 balls.

Variations:

1. No balls in the middle zone. Both teams have 10 balls and have to place as many balls as possible in the opponent's zone. If the ball leaves the outer zone, it can be brought back.

    - Develops the players' ability to pass with the right speed.

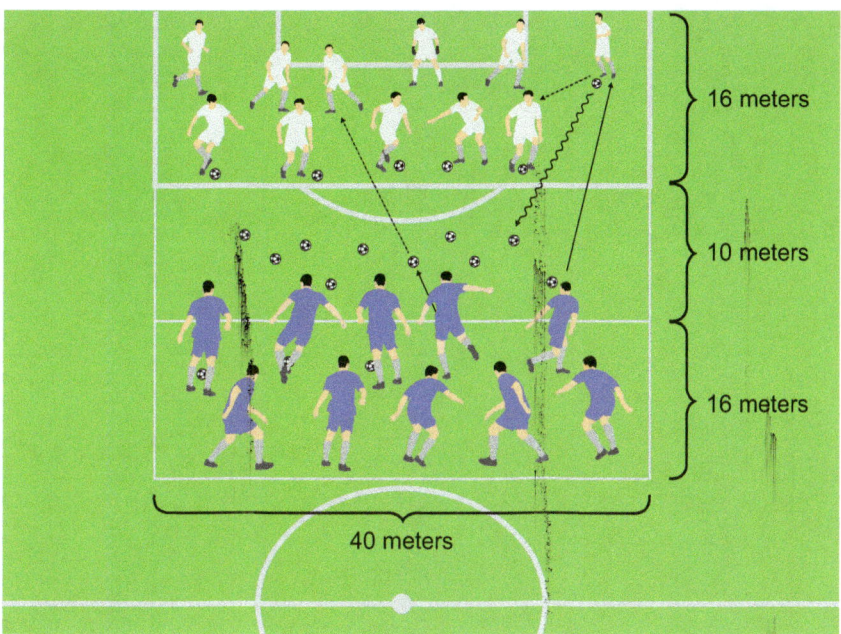

FIGURE 4.2 Hit the ball.

2. Only one touch (i.e., first time shoot/pass).

    • Becomes more difficult.

Hints:

- Fun activity.
- Players should be encouraged to hit the balls arriving before leaving the middle zone.

Drill 3: Circuit

This drill focuses on the development of technical and agility skills of youth players. The players follow the circuit and complete 2–4 circuits with progressively increased speed, separated by a break of 30 seconds.

Age group: 10–14 years.
Preparation for: Tactical training, technical training, speed training and aerobic training.
Technical elements: Dribbling and passing/shooting.
Players: 10 (1–15).
Dimension: 20 m × 30 m (see Figure 4.3).
Organization: The players are starting at different positions.
Equipment: 10 balls and 25 cones.

36 Characteristics of Warm-Up

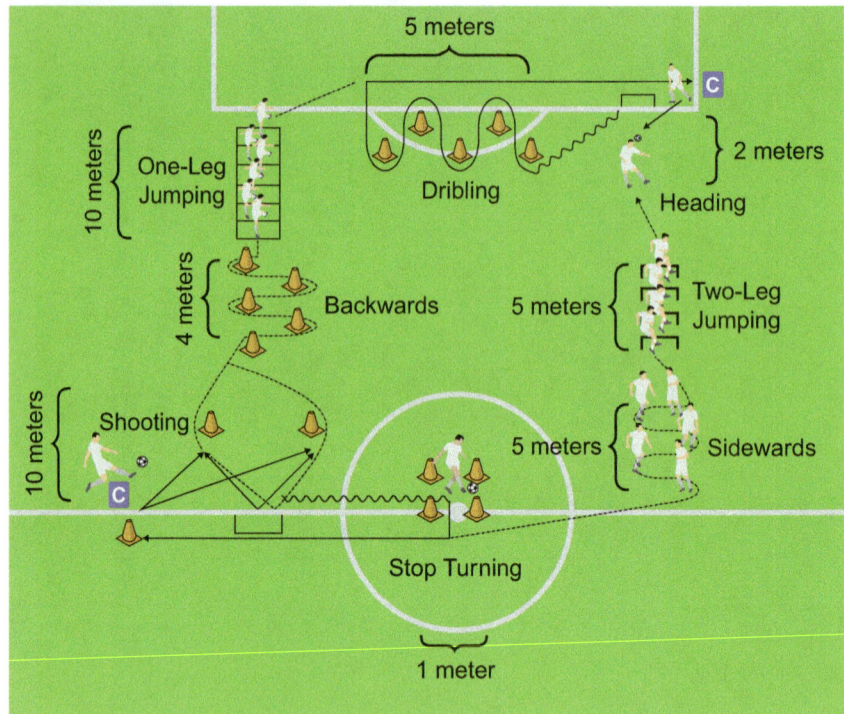

FIGURE 4.3 Circuit.

Variation:

1. Each player has a ball. If obstacles are executed without the ball, the ball is played to the end of the given obstacle, and the player continues with the ball after completing the given obstacle. At the obstacles the ball is played to the coach before receiving it and either shooting or heading.

Hints:

- The obstacles should be executed with high speed, whereas the speed between the obstacles is low and in the final rounds moderate.

Drill 4: Technical

This program lasts 16 minutes and aims to improve dribbling skills. It is particularly useful for youth players, but adult players can also benefit from these technical elements.

Age group: 10–15 years.
Preparation for: Tactical training, technical training, aerobic training, speed endurance training, speed training and agility training, power training and games.
Technical elements: Dribbling, feinting and stopping.
Players: 20 (3–30).

Dimension: A full pitch (see Figure 4.4).
Organization: Each player starts with a ball in the penalty area.
Equipment: 20 balls.

0–6 Minutes: Dribbling

Variations:

1. The players dribble among each other.
2. Players dribble to the middle circle or penalty area when the coach points in that direction, and activity continues in the given area.

Various types of dribbling:

- With one foot (left/right).
- Dribbling with the inner or outer side of the foot.
- Dribbling backward with the sole of the foot.
- Dribble and turn every 5 meters.
- Feint every 10 meters.

FIGURE 4.4 Technical.

38 Characteristics of Warm-Up

Hints:

- Only brief stops for instruction.
- Frequency of runs between zones determines the intensity.
- First phase at moderate speed. Progressively increase the speed.
- Develops the ability to perceive when controlling the ball. Watch the other players.

6–10 Minutes: Activities With Ball

- Right and then left foot on the ball. 10 repetitions.
- Right and then left knee on one ball. Move and find another ball to repeat. 6 repetitions.
- Jump over the ball forward/backward. 6 repetitions.
- Jump over the ball sideways. 6 repetitions.
- Juggling shift:
    - Left and right foot. 6 repetitions.
    - Foot and thigh. 6 repetitions.
    - Leg and head. 6 repetitions.

10–13 Minutes: High-Speed Running

Stop the ball in the air with the given body part and then sprint with the ball:

- Wrist.
- Chest and then foot.
- Head and then foot.

Hints:

- When stopping the ball, it should be controlled and moved forward in the direction of the sprint.
- The acceleration should be progressively increased.

13–16 Minutes: Challenge

All players are in the penalty area. Kick the ball of the other players out of the area with control of the player's own ball. Run at high speed to get the ball.

Hints:

- When losing the ball, acceleration should be maximal.

Summary

Warm-up of youth players should include agility and technical drills with progressively increased speed.

PART II
Warm-Up for Training and Testing

Warm-up for training can be done in many different and effective ways, and it is important to choose a program that fits the actual situation. Sometimes it may be most efficient to conduct the warm-up without the ball, but generally the coach should include the ball as much as possible to motivate the players and also to develop their technical and tactical abilities. The programs presented in the following chapters cover all situations and also warm-up for testing.

5
PREPARATION FOR TRAINING

A training session should start with a warm-up period, which may rather be called a preparation period, as the aim of the activities is to prepare the players for the specific content of the training session. For example, the warm-up for a power training session should be different from a warm-up for a tactical session. In the former, the specific muscles used in the training should be carefully warmed up, whereas the warm-up for the tactical session should include ball exercises. The benefit of doing some dynamic stretching before the actual warm-up is also discussed. The following chapters present a number of warm-up programs, and for each of them it is specified for which type of training they can be used. In each program, the intensity is progressively increased in order not to overload the players in the beginning and to gradually build up the right muscle temperature.

In order to rapidly find the right warm-up program to prepare the players for the first part of the training session, relevant warm-up programs are shown in this table according to different themes (for definitions, see Bangsbo 2007).

Aerobic training	Page 83, 85, 86, 88, 91, 95, 99, 102, 106, 108, 110, 111, 113
Speed endurance training	Page 85, 86, 106, 113
Speed and agility training	Page 106, 113, 116
Power training	Page 75, 129
Tactical training	Page 83, 85, 86, 88, 91, 95, 99, 102, 106, 108, 110, 111, 113
Technical training	Page 83, 85, 86, 88, 91, 95, 99, 102, 106, 108, 110, 111, 113

Pre-activation

"Pre-activation" is a new way of preparing for football training and match that has gained popularity in recent years. It is conducted before the warm-up program and consists of exercises that activate and stretch the muscles.

Specific glute activation warm-ups have been found to increase force production of the glutes and hamstrings and lead to improved explosive power output as well as acceleration performance. In addition, players feel more ready for training and match, and it seems to reduce the number of injuries.

A possible explanation for this relationship may be that pre-activation exercises (i.e., specific movement patterns) improve muscle activation coordination and benefit proprioception, allowing for a more optimum switch from eccentric to concentric muscle contractions.

The exercises in pre-activation are performed with low resistance either with the body or mini-bands/rubber bands as the loading. It may also include foam rolling, a self-massage technique on cylindrical muscle rollers that has an impact on flexibility, as the rolling causes the muscles to reduce the level of tension.

The pre-activation period should also include injury prevention exercises and individual exercises in relation to previous injuries. Two pre-activation programs are presented here.

Program 1: Complete

0–5 Minutes: Foam Rolling

Foam rolling of the calves, hamstrings, quadriceps, iliotibial bands, glutes and lower back. The weight of the body is used to put focused pressure on the different muscle groups. Divide the muscle in small sections and give each section a few passes up and down, move onto the next one, and then finish off by giving the entire length of the muscle a pass over. When an area is painful or tight, pause here and try to relax, roll it for 5–30 seconds and the muscle should release. 30–60 seconds per muscle group.

5–8 Minutes: Hip and Glute Activation

1. *Mini-band exercises*: Wrap the mini-band around the feet or the legs according to the exercises here. All movements should be smooth and controlled. Take a short rest in between the exercises.

- *Lateral walk*: Place the mini-band on the forefront of the feet and walk sideways while moving in a controlled fashion, avoiding any up-and-down motion. Both directions. 30 seconds.

- *Zig-zag*: Place the mini-band above the ankles and walk in a zig-zag pattern with tension in the hips by keeping tension on the band. Move forward, then backward. 30 seconds.

- *Squat*: Place the mini-band right below the knees and go to a 90-degree squat position while pressing out the knees both downward and upward. 30 seconds.

- *Reach*: Place the mini-band below the calves and reach to the front, to the top corner, to the side, to the bottom corner and to the back. The supporting leg should be completely stable throughout the exercise. 30 seconds on each leg.

46 Warm-Up for Training and Testing

8–11 Minutes: Ankle Activation

2. *Star jump*: Jump forward, backward and to both sides with one foot, then with the other foot. 8 repetitions.

3. *Scarecrow*: 3–5 standing high knees, then jump as high as possible and land on one foot to gain balance. Repeat and land on the other foot. 8 repetitions.

4. *Airplane*: Stand with right hand reaching up; bend the hip and move the right hand toward the left foot while lifting the right leg to a horizontal position and keeping the left leg straight for balance. Change sides. 12 repetitions.

5. *Walking backward lunge*: Take a large step back with left leg and sink into a lunge position. Reach behind with the right hand and touch the left heel. Move backward to stand up and repeat with the other leg. 12 repetitions.

48 Warm-Up for Training and Testing

6. *Single-leg glute bridge*: Lie on the back with the left knee bent to 90 degrees. Drive the right leg upward and bring the hips off the floor. Hold and return to start position. 2 × 20 seconds (both sides).

11–14 Minutes: Core and Upper Body Activation

7. *Handwalk*: Stand up straight; bend over and touch the floor. Walk with the hands until a push-up position is reached. Walk the feet all the way to the hands. Walk out again to loosen the stretch. Repeat the movement. 5 repetitions.

Preparation for Training 49

8. *Thumbs up*: Lie face down with hands to the side and thumbs pointing up; contract the back and move thumbs toward each other. 20 repetitions.

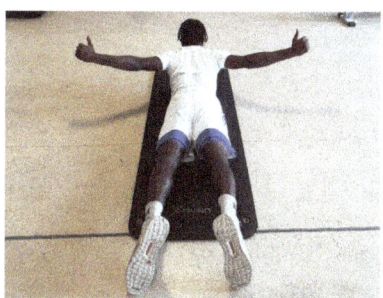

9. *Kneeling superman*: Standing on all fours (knees under hips and hands under shoulders), lift arms and legs diagonally. Make sure to keep balance. 20 repetitions.

Program 2: Condensed

0–4 Minutes: Hip, Core and Upper Body Activation

1. *Push-up plank with diagonal lift*: Start in a push-up position in a straight line from head to feet. Keeping the body still throughout the movement, lift one arm and opposite leg. Repeat, lifting opposite arm and leg. 1 minute.

2. *Lying superman*: Lie face down with the head in a neutral position and with extended arms above the head. Simultaneously lift both arms and both legs as high as possible. 1 minute.

3. *Ball squeeze*: Lie on the back with a ball between the ankles. Keeping the legs straight, tighten the abdominal muscles and squeeze the ball with the feet. Hold this position for a couple of seconds. Relax the muscles and repeat. 1 minute.

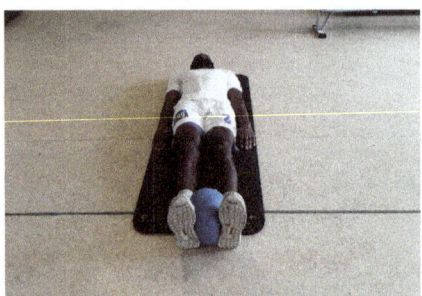

4–8 Minutes: Quadriceps and Hamstring Activation

4. *Bridge*: Lie on the back with knees bent and feet flat on the floor. Lift hips up into a bridge position and contract the glutes. Holding the hips up high, raise up on the toes and hold for 2 seconds. Keep the shoulders on the mat, and lower feet and hips back down. Repeat the exercise, keeping the hips level at all times. 1 minute.

5. *Single-leg squat*: Standing up straight on a step, possibly with some support on the side. With feet hip-width apart, keep a straight back and move the weight onto one leg. Bend the other leg and push the buttocks back behind the body. When the thigh on the step is horizontal, move the lowered leg back up on the step and repeat. 6 repetitions on each leg.

6. *Nordic hamstring*: Kneel on a soft surface. The body should be straight from the shoulders to the knees throughout the exercise. Lean forward as far as possible while controlling the movement with tension on hamstrings and gluteal muscles. When the position can no longer be held, take the weight of the fall on the hands. 6 repetitions.

7. *Reverse Nordic*: Kneel on a mat on legs that are shoulder-width apart. Cross the arms over the chest, and squeeze the glutes and abdominal muscles. Keeping hips pushed forward in line with shoulders and knees, slowly lean back over the calves. Do not allow the hips to drop down, and return to the starting position at a slow and steady pace. 6 repetitions.

Summary

Pre-activation is conducted before the warm-up program and consists of exercises with low resistance, either with the body or mini-bands/rubber bands as the loading. This will activate and stretch the muscles and likely lead to improved coordination of muscle activity during football training and match. The method has gained popularity in recent years, as the players feel more ready for training and it seems to reduce the number of injuries. Pre-activation should also include exercises in relation to players' previous injuries.

Bibliography

Bangsbo J. *Aerobic and anaerobic training in soccer.* www.soccerfitness.expert, 2007.

Buckthorpe M, Wright S, Bruce-Low S, Nanni G, Sturdy T, Gross AS, Bowen L, Styles B, Della Villa S, Davison M, Gimpel M. Recommendations for hamstring injury prevention in elite football: translating research into practice. *British Journal of Sports Medicine* 53: 449–456, 2019.

Crow JF, Buttifant D, Kearny SG, Hrysomallis C. Low load exercises targeting the gluteal muscle group acutely enhance explosive power output in elite athletes. *Journal of Strength and Conditioning Research* 26, 2: 438–442, 2012.

6

WARM-UP WITHOUT THE BALL

Warming up without the ball is a basic and controlled way to start a training session, which may reduce the risk of injuries caused by sudden movements that the body is not prepared for. Furthermore, the players can adjust their effort according to their individual needs. There is also a psychological aspect to warm up without the ball, as the players may talk and joke while jogging or performing exercises that they know well.

The specific exercises chosen for warm-up without the ball may depend on weather conditions and temperature. In rainy weather, exercises lying down or sitting should be avoided. Likewise, in a cold and windy environment, focus should be on exercises that markedly raise the body temperature and motivation of the players.

The day before a match, a program with dynamic stretching exercises may be selected (see Program 3, page 67), whereas exercises that make the muscles relax are preferred the day after a match or a hard training session (see Program 2, page 60). During weekly training, warm-up without the ball can also be used to complement the power training, whereby exercises for injury prevention, balance and power are incorporated (see Program 4, page 75).

Warm-up without the ball may be followed by warm-up with the ball. Thus, the programs presented can be used alone or in combination with parts of the programs presented in Chapter 7.

A selection of programs is provided here. Each lasts 10–15 minutes and prepares the body for training in a controlled manner. The first program contains various activities and running. The other programs consist of dynamic stretches and exercises for balance and strength that are followed by a few minutes of activities and running from the first program. Before doing warm-up with the ball, it is recommended to do some of the exercises from the first program for a few minutes.

Program 1: Activities and Running

This warm-up program is useful when it is cold or when there is a need for a time-efficient warm-up, as the program lasts approximately 10 minutes. Activities and running are interspersed such that activities are carried out while moving from one side of the pitch to midway, and running is performed from midway to the other side of the pitch (see Figure 6.1).

54 Warm-Up for Training and Testing

FIGURE 6.1 Activities and running.

1. *Butt kicks*: Heels touch the glutes.

2. *High knees*: Move the knees are horizontal (one at a time).

3. *Skips*: Pull the knee to the chest, and use arms actively to contribute to each skip.

4. *Fast feet forward*: Make quick and short movements of the feet, moving in a zig-zag pattern.

5. *Backward running*: Run backward; look over the shoulder to orientate.

56 Warm-Up for Training and Testing

6. *Backward butt kicks*: Same as "butt kicks," but backward.

7. *Backward high knees*: Same as "high knees," but backward.

8. *Backward slalom*: Run backward while slaloming.

Warm-Up Without the Ball **57**

9. *Fast feet backward*: Same as "fast feet," but backward; look over the shoulder to orientate.

10. *Sidesteps*: Move sideways with a low center of gravity. Change sides after 3 repetitions.

11. *Carioca with high step in front (moving left)*: Moving sideways, the right leg changes between stepping in front and back of the left leg. When in front, the knee is pulled up to a 90-degree angle at the beginning of the step; the hip is twisted and the knee is brought down at the end of the step.

58 Warm-Up for Training and Testing

12. *Carioca with high step in front (moving right)*: Moving sideways, the left leg changes between stepping in front and back of the right leg. When in front, the knee is pulled up to a 90-degree angle at the beginning of the step; the hip is twisted and the knee is brought down at the end of the step.

13. *Headers*: Perform jumps for a pretend header, alternating between jumps on right, left and both legs.

14. *N sprints*: Sprint forward 10 meters, turn and sprint 5 meters in the opposite direction, turn and sprint 10 meters.

15. *Lightning sprints*: Sprint forward 10 meters, decelerate, take 2–3 steps backward, then sprint forward 10 meters.

16. *Zorro sprints*: Sprint 3–5 meters in each direction, creating a "Z" (plant right, plant left, plant right *or* plant left, plant right, plant left).

17. *Backward sprints*: Backward sprint 5 meters, turn and sprint forward 10 meters.

60 Warm-Up for Training and Testing

Program 2: On the Ground

This comprehensive program lasts 15 minutes and is recommended to be performed on days where a thorough warm-up is a priority. It is recommended to use a mat if the pitch is wet. The exercises in the program consist of dynamic stretches, exercises that target core stability and balance, and some exercises for activation and strength.

0–12 Minutes: Dynamic Stretching, Core and Balance, Muscle Activation and Strength

1. *Hip rotation, knees together*: While sitting with knees together, move the legs from side to side. 30 seconds.

2. *Hip rotation, knees apart*: While sitting with knees apart, move the legs from side to side with the insides of the knees touching the ground. 30 seconds.

3. *90/90 hamstring stretch*: Lie on the back with one leg flat on the ground and the other having a 90-degree angle in hip and knee; hands are locked behind the knee; straighten the leg. 10 repetitions.

4. *Hip crossover*: Lie on the back, with both legs in the air (90-degree angle in the hips). Use the abs to move the legs from side to side without the feet touching the ground, while relaxing the neck. Place arms on the ground to the sides to ensure stability. 30 seconds.

5. *T stretch*: Lie on the back with arms pointing to the sides. Roll hips from side to side as the right foot moves to the left hand, then the left foot moves to the right arm. 30 seconds.

6. *Back stretch*: Lie on the back; right hand goes to the outside of the left knee, which is bent and moved slightly upward; left knee is pulled toward the ground so the hip rotates. Left hand is flat on the ground and to the side. 3 × 10 seconds each side.

7. *Straight-leg sit-up*: From a flat position on the back with arms above the head, move the upper body to a straight position (90 degrees in the hip), moving arms back to increase the stretch. 10 repetitions.

8. *Abductor leg lift*: Keep body straight on the side, including the (lower) arm, which is straight; the head rests on the lower arm. With the lower feet flexed, lift the upper leg and lower slowly, creating resistance on the way down. 30 seconds each side.

9. *Pendulum*: Keep body straight on the side, including the (lower) arm, which is straight; the head rests on the lower arm. Move the upper leg forward (foot flexed) and backward (feet extended), like a pendulum. 30 seconds each side.

10. *Clam*: Keep upper body straight on the side, including the (lower) arm, which is straight; the head rests on the lower arm. Knees are bent. While keeping the feet together, raise and lower the upper leg. 30 seconds each side.

11. *Scorpion*: Point arms to the side. Move the feet from side to side; move the right heel toward the left hand, then move the left heel toward the right hand. 30 seconds.

12. *Abdominal stretch*: With arms below the shoulders, press the upper body away from the surface to straighten arms. Hip is loose. 6 × 5 seconds.

13. *Superman*: Lift arms and legs diagonally. Make sure to keep balance. 30 seconds.

14. *Leg lift*: Standing on all fours, lift one leg (bent) so the thigh is horizontal and the shin vertical (90-degree angle in the knee). From this position, lift and lower the leg. 30 seconds each side.

15. *Calf stretch*: Standing on all fours, push back so the butt is lifted into the air and only hands and toes are touching the ground. Press the heel of one foot toward the surface while resting the other foot on the opposite calf. 6 × 5 seconds each side.

16. *Hip raise*: Move the heels toward the butt; from this position, raise the hips (performing the exercise on one leg at a time makes it more difficult). Raise hips as high as possible, squeezing the glutes. 10 repetitions on each side.

17. *Active bridge*: From a regular bridge position, raise the body on the arms (either one at a time or both simultaneously). 30 seconds.

18. *Active side bridge*: From a side-bridge position, move the hips up and down. Raise the hips as high as possible (they will come down on their own!). 30 seconds each side.

19. *Combination stretch*: Starting from a push-up position, move the chest toward the ground (without touching), then raise the chest and loosen the hip to stretch the abs. Return to the push-up position. Next, move one leg to the hand on the same side, lift the upper body to a vertical position, and reach the arms to the sides while turning the to the side of the leg in front to stretch the hip. Return to push-up position and repeat on the other side. Return to push-up position. 6 repetitions.

12–15 Minutes: Activities and Running

For the final 3 minutes of the warm-up, perform some activities and running from Program 1 ("Activities and Running").

Program 3: Standing

The program lasts around 10 minutes and consists of stretches that are performed while moving. Some are performed while walking (players move into the stretch), called "walking stretches"; others are performed dynamically (swinging movements) and are called "dynamic stretches." Overall, the exercises activate and improve flexibility of muscles and joints. The program is recommended for wet or cold conditions when lying and sitting should be avoided.

0–4 Minutes: Walking Stretches

Players move from one side of the pitch to the other, and stretches (or positions) are held for 2–3 seconds:

1. *Combination stretch*: From a standing position, take a large step forward with the left leg. Place the right hand on the ground aligned with the left foot (shoulder-width apart); move the left hand between the legs and grab the outside of the ankle on the left foot; the inside will be stretched (the stretch will increase by twisting the torso). Next, place the left hand next to the left foot (which is now between the two hands). Then move the butt backward and lift the toes on the left foot, which creates a stretch on the backside. Lift both arms and the upper body becomes vertical to stretch the hip (pointing the arm to the left will increase the stretch). During the whole stretch, the back leg is straight; the body is moved to the starting position and the stretch is repeated on the other side. 3 repetitions on each side.

68 Warm-Up for Training and Testing

2. *Sumo squat*: From a standing position, move the feet to a wide stance and move to a squat position with straight arms on the inside of the thighs. Grab the toes (high chest) with the fingers while looking to the sky. Next, look between the legs while straightening (stretching) the legs as much as possible. 10 repetitions.

Warm-Up Without the Ball **69**

3. *Quads*: Pull one leg close by grabbing just above the wrist, thereby standing on one leg. 10 repetitions.

4. *Static hamstrings*: One leg is positioned in front of the other; bend the back leg, keeping the back straight. 10 repetitions.

5. *Static insides*: With one leg straight on the ground, take a step to the opposite side and bend the knee. The back is straight. 10 repetitions.

6. *Glutes*: While grabbing the ankle and the knee, pull the leg toward the chest to create a stretch of the gluteus and iliotibial band. 10 repetitions.

7. *Static hips*: Step with one leg into a half lunge and twist the upper body in the opposite direction to stretch the hip. To increase the stretch, move the arms to the opposite side of the back leg; the glute of the back leg is contracted. 5 repetitions for each leg.

4–7 Minutes: Dynamic Stretching

Players move from one side of the pitch to the other while performing the following dynamic stretches:

8. *Hip out*: Pull the knee toward the chest and move it to the side as far as possible; lower the leg, working the opposite abductor. 10 repetitions.

72 Warm-Up for Training and Testing

9. *Hip in*: Pull the knee out and up, then move it in (while still in the air); lower the leg, working the opposite leg adductor. 10 repetitions.

10. *Forward kick*: Keeping the body straight, perform a forward kick with a straight leg and extended foot. Clapping under the knee will increase the stretch. 10 repetitions.

Warm-Up Without the Ball 73

11. *Forward kick with a twist*: Keeping the body straight, perform a forward kick with a twist. 10 repetitions.

12. *Leg extension stretch*: Move the knee toward the chest; kick the leg out and down. 10 repetitions.

13. *Insides*: Keeping the body and leg straight, kick to the side. 10 repetitions.

14. *Hips*: Keeping the body and leg straight, kick the leg back and pull the opposite arm toward the back leg. 10 repetitions.

7–10 Minutes: Activities and Running

For the final 3 minutes of the warm-up, perform some activities and running from Program 1 ("Activities and Running").

Program 4: Balance and Strength

This program lasts 13 minutes and incorporates exercises to challenge balance and strength. It can, therefore, be useful to perform this program during periods where power training is not performed, such as during a tight match schedule.

0–6 Minutes: Balance

All exercises are performed while moving (walking or jumping) across the pitch.

1. *Hand walk*: From a standing position, bend and reach toward the surface with the hands. In small increments, move the hands forward as far as possible (without tumbling); legs must be straight; glutes and core muscles must be activated. Then, by small steps driven by the ankles, move the feet all the way to the hands (legs should remain straight). 6 repetitions.

2. *Airplane*: Straighten one arm and reach for the toes of the opposite foot. Move the other leg toward a horizontal position. Change sides and repeat. 10 repetitions.

3. *Single leg squat*: Squat as far down as possible without losing balance. Change legs and repeat. 10 repetitions.

4. *Walking lunge*: Take a step back to drop into a lunge, using the arms for balance. From here, step all the way into a forward lunge. Change sides and repeat. 10 repetitions.

5. *T ankle jump*: Jump on one leg at a time. An easy jump forward (a) is followed by an easy jump to one side (b) followed by a maximum jump to the opposite side (c) and back to center (d), thereby completing a "T" movement pattern. Change legs and repeat. 10 repetitions.

6. *Squat jump:* From a standing position, move down to a squat position. Then jump slightly forward and upward. Go straight back to squat position when landing. 10 repetitions.

7. *Broad jump*: From a standing position, jump as far as possible. Perform a countermovement (knees bent) before takeoff and during landing. Three jumps are performed in a row (the controlled landing in between gives a transition phase of about 1–2 seconds). 5 repetitions.

8. *Header jump*: Take one or more steps forward and jump as high as possible on one leg and do a pretend header. Switch and jump on the other leg. 10 repetitions.

9. *Contact jump*: Players are together in pairs. Both players jump at the same time and make shoulder contact. Keep balance when landing; however, balance should be challenged, for example, by landing on one leg. 6 repetitions.

6–10 Minutes: Strength

Exercises are performed twice in the following order:

10. *Bridge*: Position front; left and right side are each held. 30 seconds.

11. *Nordic hamstring*: Players are together in pairs. One player lies face down while the other player sits on the calves. The player on the ground pushes off the ground, creating a 90-degree angle in the knees. Next the player moves forward while trying not to tip. When the body tips, hands are moved to the ground to stop the movement of the upper body. Glutes must be contracted throughout the movement. 5 repetitions for each player.

12. *Thumbs up*: Lying face down with hands to the side and thumbs pointing up, contract the back and move the thumbs toward each other. 20 repetitions.

13. *Scissor sit-up*: Lying on the back with arms straight over the head, move the hands to touch just above the ankles at the same time as the legs are lifted above the ground. 20 repetitions.

82 Warm-Up for Training and Testing

14. *5–5–5*: 5 repetitions each of push-ups, where (a) hands are on top of each other, (b) hands are below the shoulders and (c) hands are placed as far out as possible. Exercises follow each other with no rest in between.

10–13 Minutes: Activities and Running

For the final 3 minutes of the warm-up, perform some activities and running from Program 1 ("Activities and Running", see page 53).

Summary

Warming up without the ball is a basic and controlled way to start a training session. Such a warm-up can be done in many ways, but to be efficient and to avoid a drop in motivation of the players, it is important to choose a program that fits the actual situation and weather conditions.

Warming up without the ball may be followed by warm-up with the ball. Thus, the programs presented can be used alone or in combination with parts of the programs presented in Chapter 7. Nevertheless, the coach should aim at including the ball as much as possible to motivate the players and also to develop their technical and tactical abilities.

7

WARM-UP WITH THE BALL

This chapter describes warm-up programs with the ball, where technical and tactical elements are integrated in the program. For these exercises, the players will have to anticipate the ball and the movements of teammates, which may create sudden movements that increase the risk of injury. Thus, it is suggested that that the players spend a few minutes doing dynamic stretches at the start of the programs.

Program 1: Pairs

This program lasts 15 minutes, and focuses on technical development within passing, stopping and controlling the ball in various situations. The difficulties of the technical elements should be modified to suit the playing level of the players.

Preparation for: Tactical training, technical training, aerobic training, speed endurance training, and games.
Technical elements: Passing and stopping.
Players: 20 (2–30).
Dimension: Half a pitch (see Figure 7.1).
Organization: Pairs (i.e., 10 pairs), with a ball at the midline.
Equipment: 10 balls.

0–10 Minutes: Technical

Players pass after a one-touch instep kick that reaches the midline. Players come closer and closer, then farther and farther away from each other. The player that is not in possession must therefore backpedal to reach the right distance.

Variations:
- Left/right foot.
- Wrist.

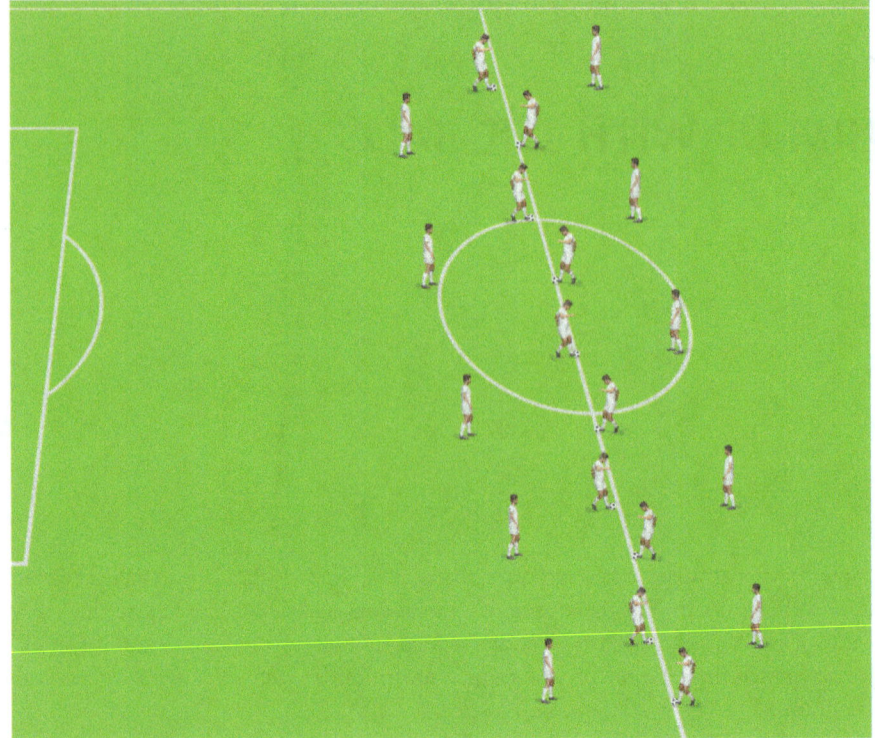

FIGURE 7.1 Pairs.

From the midline, one player runs forward and the other backward. When reaching the penalty area, they run back to midline (i.e., now the other player runs forward). The player running backward throws the ball and the other player does the following actions:

- Heads back.
- Passes with the inside of the foot, alternating left and right foot.
- Passes with wrist, alternating left and right foot.
- Stops with wrist, thigh and chest, and then passes back, alternating left and right leg.

Hints:

- Focus on the execution of the heading, passing and stopping.

10–12 Minutes: Juggling

Players keep the ball in the air, alternating left and right legs with exactly one, two or three touches.

Hints:

- Focus on balance when joggling.

12–15 Minutes: High-Speed Running (Free Space)

- One player dribbles and overtakes the other player with high speed; the other player runs in the same direction and passes with the heel to the other player, who takes the ball and overtakes with high speed and then passes with the heel, and so on.
- One player passes to the other player, who turns and slowly dribbles until being overtaken with high speed by the player, who then turns and receives the ball and turns to dribble slowly, and so on.
- One player throws the ball over the head of the other player, who turns and gets the ball and returns at high speed, and so on.

Hints:

- No stops to instruct.
- Intensity is progressively increased.

Program 2: Collaboration

This program lasts 13 minutes and has a significant number of basic tactical elements. Thus, it is ideal to improve the players' tactical understanding.

Preparation for: Tactical training, technical training, aerobic training, speed endurance training, speed and agility training, and games.
Technical elements: Dribbling, passing and stopping.
Tactical elements: Move in free space, wall pass and overlap.
Players: 20 (3–30).
Dimension: A full pitch (see Figure 7.2).
Organization: Each second player in the penalty area with a ball.
Equipment: 10 balls.

0–10 Minutes: Passing

- All players are inside the penalty area and either dribbling or jogging. All players run to the middle circle or opposite penalty area when the coach points in the direction, and below activities continues in that area.

With eye contact between two players:

- Run in free space and receive the ball.
- Takeover (i.e., the player without the ball continues with the ball).
- Overlap and pass.
- Stop the ball in the air with the chest (or thigh) and dribble.
- Heel kick after players pass each other.
- Wall pass. Change every 30 seconds.
- Return the ball in the air with a header. Change every 30 seconds.

FIGURE 7.2 Collaboration.

Hints:

- Only brief stops to instruct the tactical elements.
- Coach execution of the technical and tactical elements.
- The frequency of runs between areas determines the intensity.
- Use moderate speed in the first phase. Progressively increase intensity.
- Develops the ability to perceive when controlling the ball. Look after the other players.

10–13 Minutes: Attacking

Players defend their ball. Players without a ball should get a ball. 45 seconds of exercise; 15 seconds of rest.

Hints:

- Encourage the players without a ball to "attack" the players with a ball.

Program 3: Couples

This program lasts 13 minutes and is focused on passing and stopping as well as controlling the ball during intense actions. Thus, it is useful to develop the players' technical qualities.

Preparation for: Tactical training, technical training, aerobic training, speed endurance training, speed and agility training, and games.
Technical elements: Passing and stopping.
Players: 16 (2–24).
Dimension: Half a pitch (see Figure 7.3).
Organization: Pairs (i.e., 8 pairs).
Equipment: 8 balls.

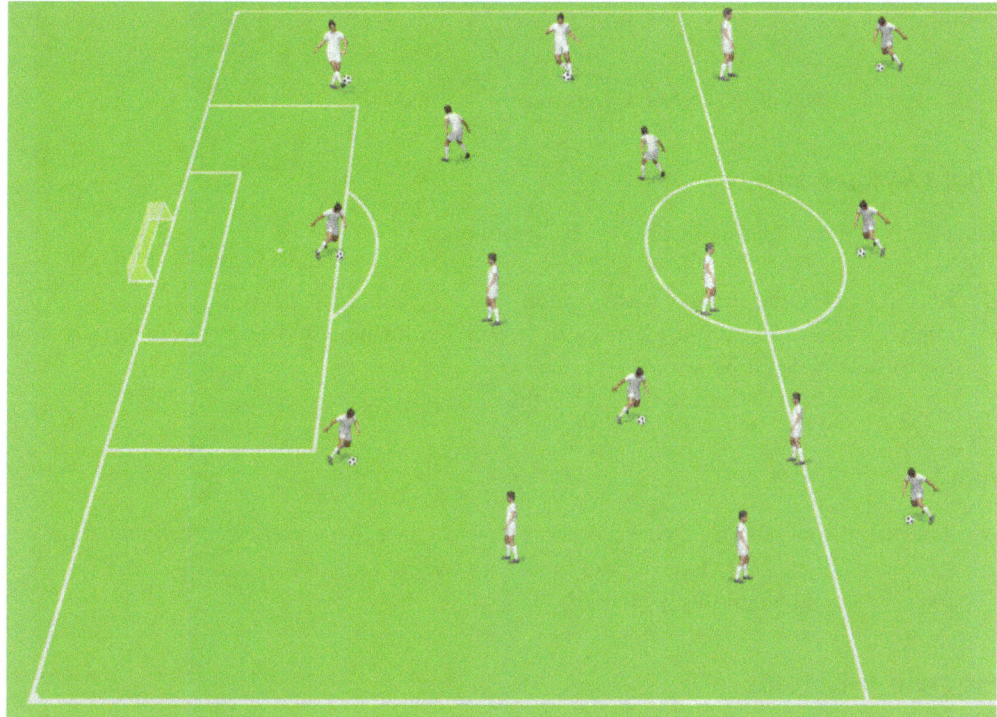

FIGURE 7.3 Couples.

0–6 Minutes: Passing

The couples move freely on the pitch, making short passes. Pass and move.

First make free touches, then exactly two touches, and lastly stop with one foot and pass with the other foot.

Hints:

- No stops to instruct.
- Coach execution of the technical elements.
- Intensity should progressively increase.

6–10 Minutes: Activities With Ball

Allow 3 meters between the couple of players. One player throws the ball, and the other player returns the ball using:

- Inside of the foot, alternating left and right.
- Head.
- Upper side of the foot, alternating left and right foot.
- Stop with thigh and chest, then pass back.

Change after 6 repetitions.

Hints:

- No stops to instruct.
- Coach execution of the technical elements.

10–13 Minutes: Intense

The players in the couple are kicking the ball every other time:

- Keep the ball in the air; only bounce once.
- High ball over the head; one player kicks the ball over the head of the other, who turns and get the ball and brings it back.
- 1 vs. 1; one player defends the ball while the other player tries to get it.

Hints:

- The players should challenge each other (e.g., in the first two exercises the ball should hit the ground at a significant distance from the other player).
- Intensity should progressively increase.

Program 4: The Line

"The line" takes 15 minutes. It is a passing drill that serves the purpose of developing the players' ability to make precise short- and medium-distance passes and to create space before receiving the ball.

Preparation for: Tactical training, technical training, aerobic training and games.
Technical elements: Strong flat passes with the inside of the foot and controlled receives to pass the ball in the next sequence.
Dimension: 40 m × 15 m per group.
Organization: Groups of 5 to 9 players.
Equipment: 1 ball and 4 cones per group.

0–3 Minutes: Activities and Jogging (Figure 7.4a)

Various activities are conducted and interchanged with jogging. Players are organized in two rows (A and B), and the front player of each row selects the exercise (see page 89) in turns, and after completing the exercise moves to the back of the row.

3–7 Minutes: Receive and Pass (Figure 7.4b)

A to B (*A to P2*), B to C (*B to P3*), C to D (*C to P4*), D dribbles to E (*D to P1*), and so on. Two touches (except when dribbling).

Hints:

- The player receiving the ball should create space by first making a movement in the opposite direction.

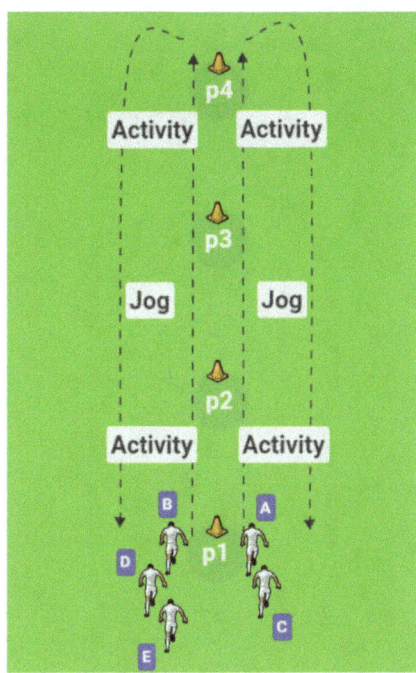

FIGURE 7.4A The line: activities and jogging.

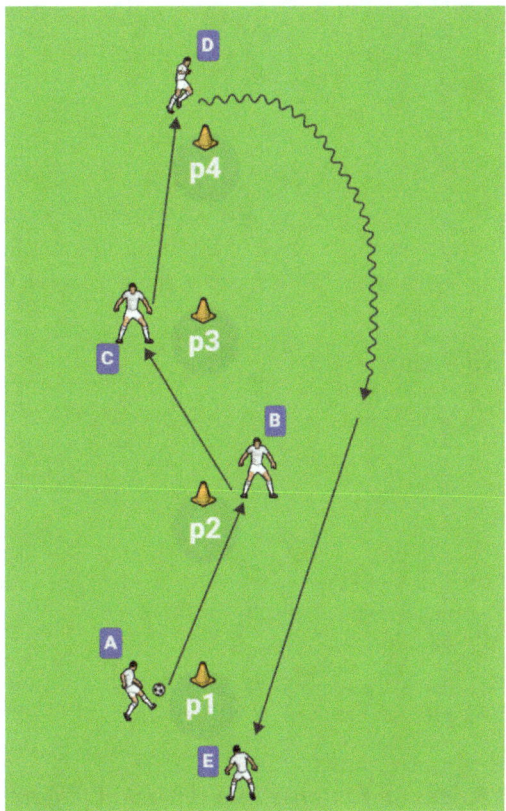

FIGURE 7.4B The line: receive and pass.

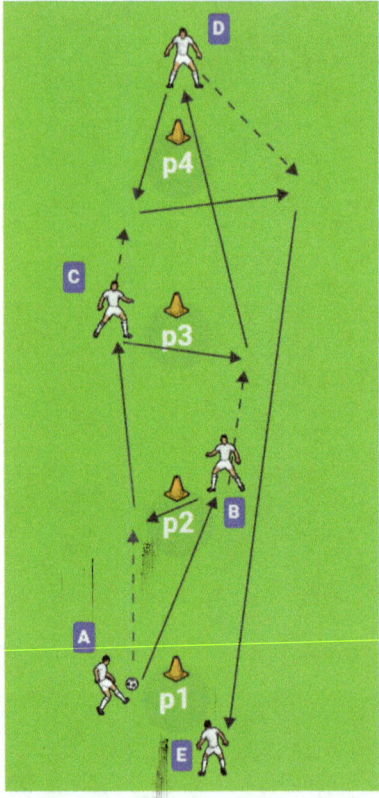

FIGURE 7.4C The line: one-two.

- Players should time movements to the pass (i.e., not stand and wait for the ball).
- Players should create "playing angles" (if B moves right, C moves left).

7–11 Minutes: One-Two (Figure 7.4c)

A to B to A to C (*A to P2*), C to B to D to C to D (*B to P3; C to P4*), D to E (*D to P1*), and so on. One touch.

Hints:

- The player receiving the ball should create space by first making a movement in the opposite direction (i.e., not stand and wait for the ball).
- Players have to time their movements to the pass.
- Players should create "playing angles" (e.g., if B moves right, C moves left).
- The first touch should be in the direction of the movement.

11–15 Minutes: Long Passes and Intense Run With Ball (Figure 7.4d)

A to C to B to D, D dribbles to E (*A to P2; B to P3; C to P4; D to P1*), and so on. One touch (except when dribbling).

Warm-Up With the Ball **91**

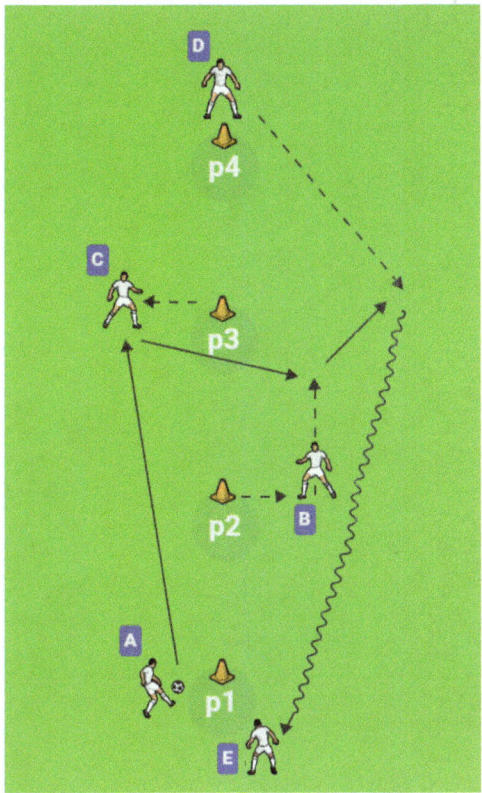

FIGURE 7.4D The line: long pass and intense run with ball.

Hints:

- The player receiving the ball should create space by first making a movement in the opposite direction (i.e., not stand and wait for the ball).
- Players should create "playing angles" (e.g., if A is left, B moves to the right and C moves to the left).
- Players should time movements to the pass.
- Dribbling should be at high speed.

Program 5: The Square

This program lasts 15 minutes. It is based on a passing drill with the purpose of developing the players' ability to make precise and strong short-distance passes and to create space before receiving the ball. The player receiving the ball should therefore create space by first making a movement in the opposite direction (i.e., not stand and wait for the ball). Also, players should time movements to the pass. If there are more than 5 players in each square, a second ball can be introduced.

Preparation for: Tactical training, technical training, aerobic training and games.
Technical elements: Strong, flat passes with the inside of the foot and controlled receives to pass the ball in next sequence.
Dimension: 20 m × 20 m per group.

92 Warm-Up for Training and Testing

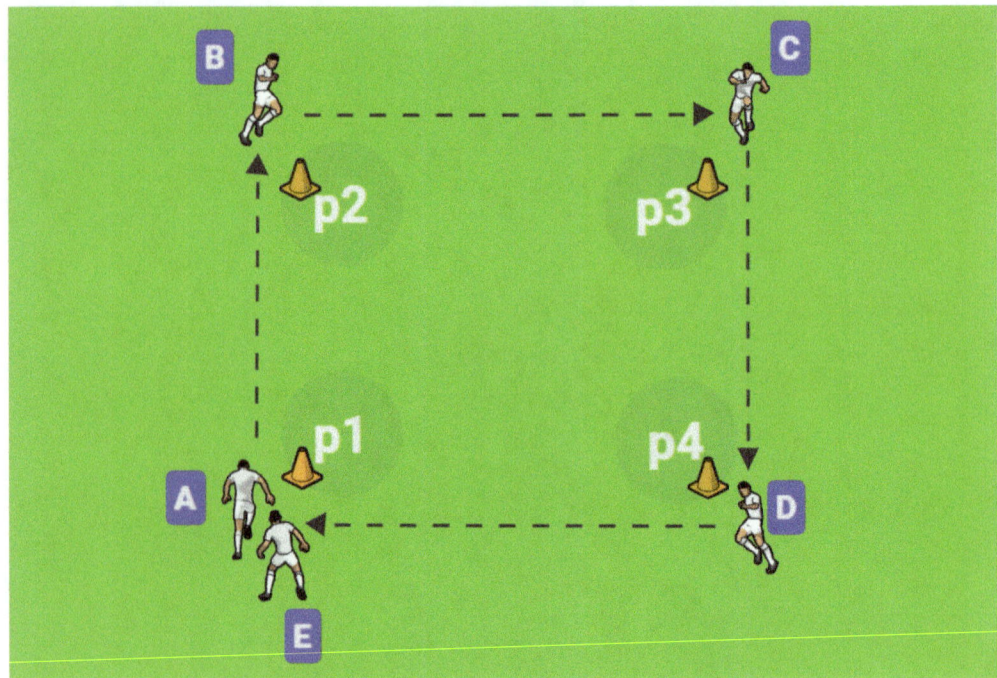

FIGURE 7.5A The square: activities and jogging.

Organization: Groups of 5 to 9 players.
Equipment: 1 ball and 4 cones per group.

0–3 Minutes: Activities and Jogging (Figure 7.5a)

An activity is performed for one side of the square and is followed by jogging for another side of the square. Players select in turn (A, then B, and so on) an exercise (see page 53). All players move at the same time.

3–6 Minutes: Dribbling (Figure 7.5b)

A to B to C to D to E (*A to P2; B to P3; C to P4; D to P1*), and so on. Players dribble, make a feint, accelerate and pass to a teammate. The direction of play changes from clockwise to counterclockwise after 90 seconds, and speed is gradually increased. This also applies to the next three drills.

6–9 Minutes: Receive and Pass (Figure 7.5c)

A to B to C to D to E (*A to P2; B to P3; C to P4; D to P1*), and so on. Two touches.

Hints:

- Passes should be received with one foot and then passed with the other foot.

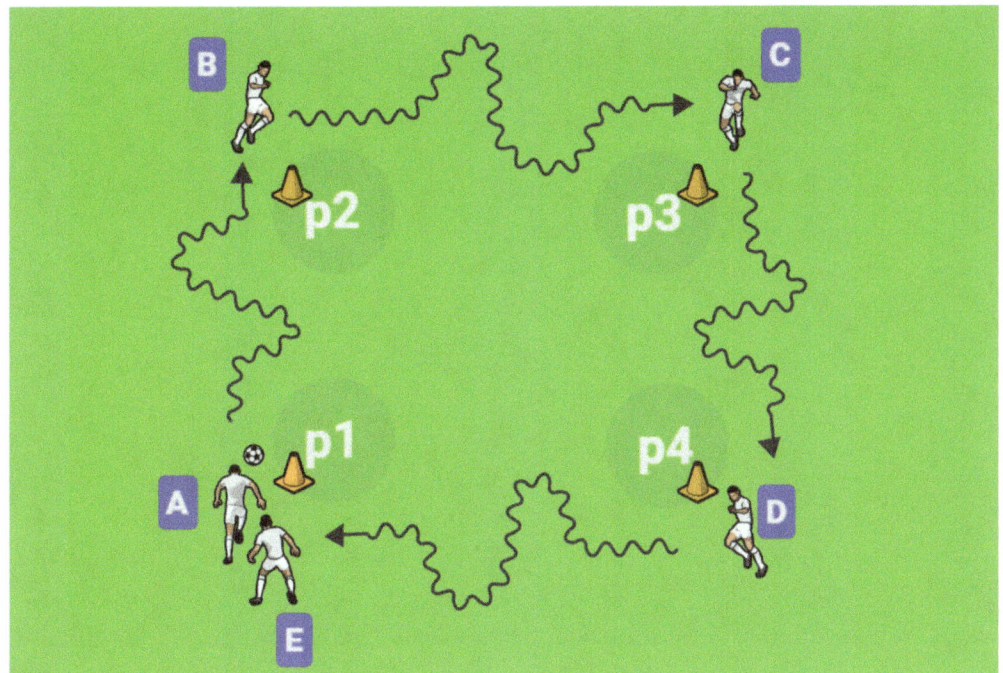

FIGURE 7.5B The square: dribbling.

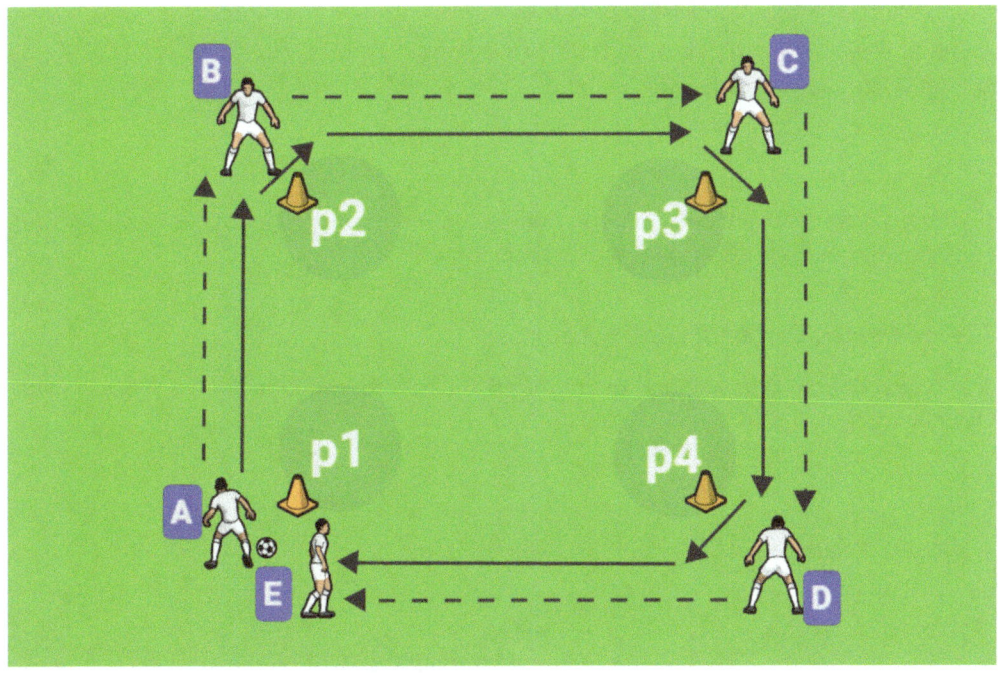

FIGURE 7.5C The square: receive and pass.

94 Warm-Up for Training and Testing

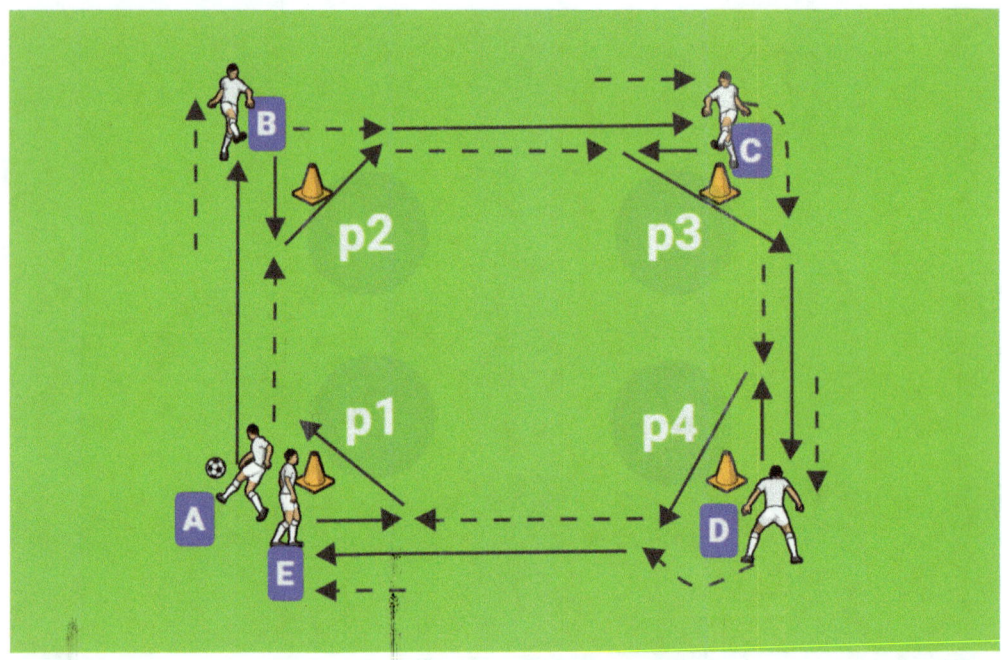

FIGURE 7.5D The square: one–two.

9–12 Minutes: One-Two (Figure 7.5d)

A to B to A to B (*A to P2*), B to C to B to C (*B to P3*), C to D to C to D (*C to P4*), D to E to D to E (*D to P1*), and so on. One touch.

Hints:

- Players make short, precise and strong passes around each cone (players move on the outside).
- Players create space by moving away from the cone.

12–15 Minutes: Diagonal (Figure 7.5e)

A to B to A to C to B (*A to P2*), B to D to C (*B to P3*), C to E to D to A (*C to P4*), and so on. One touch.

Hints:

- Players should receive and pass the ball with the outside leg.

Warm-Up With the Ball **95**

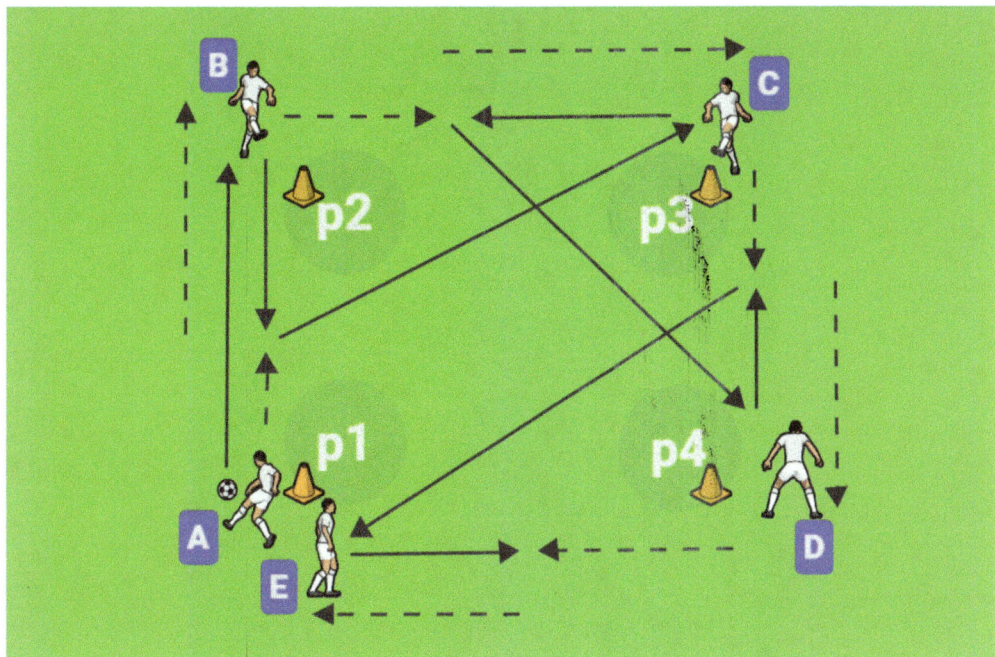

FIGURE 7.5E The square: diagonal.

Program 6: The Triangle

The "triangle" program lasts 15 minutes. It is a passing drill that develops the players' ability to make precise and strong short-distance passes and to create space before receiving the ball, and to play a fast passing game.

Preparation for: Tactical training, technical training, aerobic training and games.
Technical elements: Strong, flat passes with the inside of the foot and controlled stopping to pass the ball in next sequence.
Dimension: 20 m × 20 m per group.
Organization: Groups of 4 to 7 players.
Equipment: 1 ball and 3 cones per group.

0–3 Minutes: Activities and Jogging (Figure 7.6a)

Various dynamic stretching exercises are performed (P1 to P2 to P3) following by jogging (P3 to P1). Players are organized in a row. The first player selects the exercise (see page 96) to be done by all players and moves to the back of the row when the triangle has been completed.

3–6 Minutes: Dribbling (Figure 7.6b)

A dribbles, makes a feint, passes to B or C (*A to P2/P3*), B or C dribbles, makes a feint, passes to D (*B/C to P1*), D dribbles, makes a feint, passes to E (*D to P1*) and so on. Speed is gradually increased, which also applies to the next three exercises.

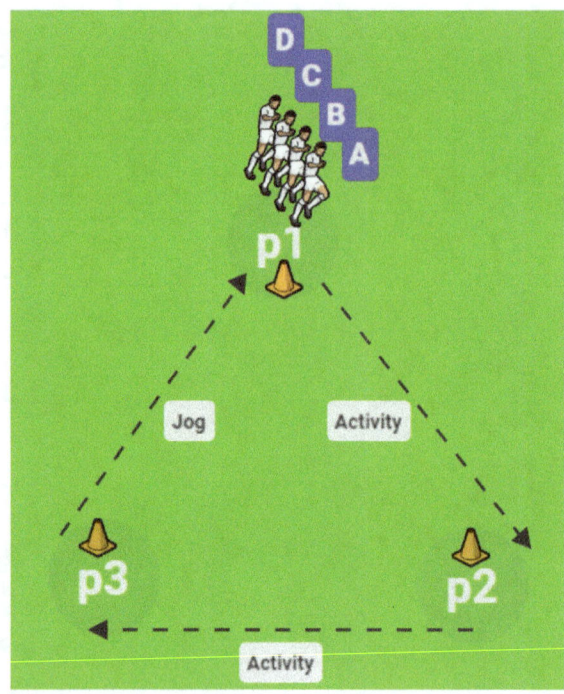

FIGURE 7.6A The triangle: activities and jogging.

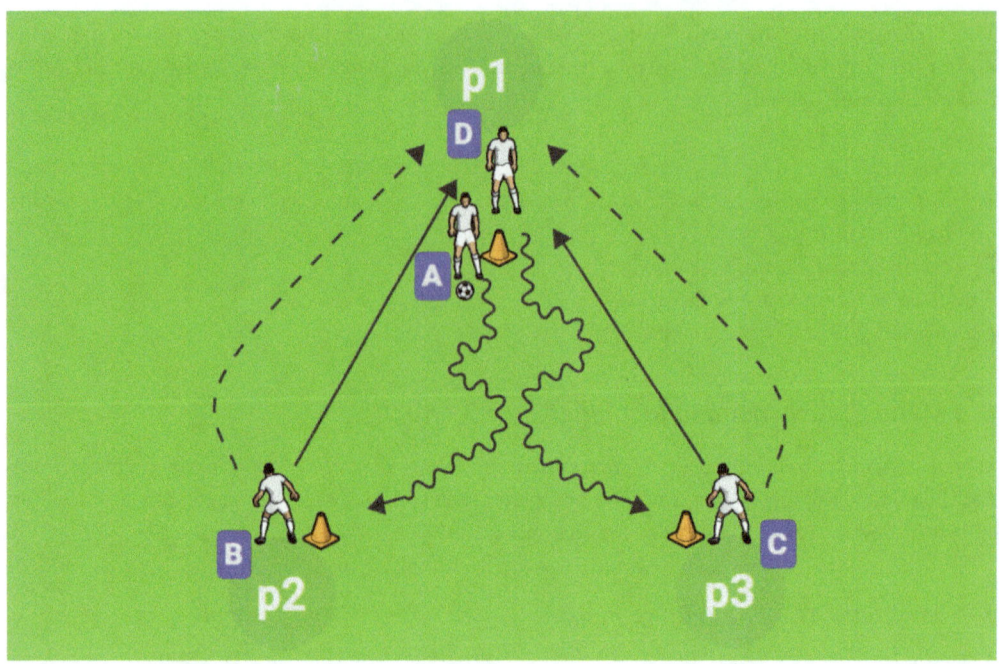

FIGURE 7.6B The triangle: dribbling.

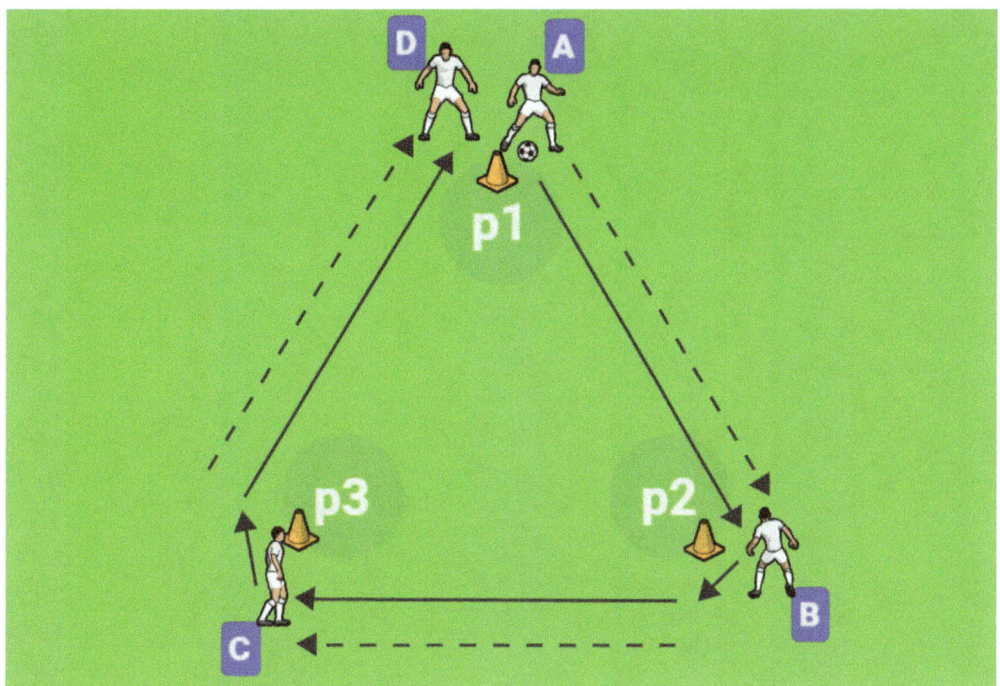

FIGURE 7.6C The triangle: receive and pass.

Hints:

- The players should accelerate after passing.

6–9 Minutes: Receive and Pass (Figure 7.6c)

A to B to C to D (*A to P2; B to P3; C to P1*), and so on. Two touches. Direction of play changes from clockwise to counterclockwise after 90 seconds. This also applies to the next two drills.

Hints:

- Players create space by moving away from the cone.
- Passes are received with one foot and then passed on with the other foot.

9–12 Minutes: One-Two (Figure 7.6d)

A to B to A to B (*A to P2*), B to C to B to C (*B to P3*), C to D to C to D (*C to P1*) and so on. One touch.

Hints:

- Players make short, precise and hard passes around each cone (players move on the outside).
- Players create space by moving away from the cone before receiving the ball.

98 Warm-Up for Training and Testing

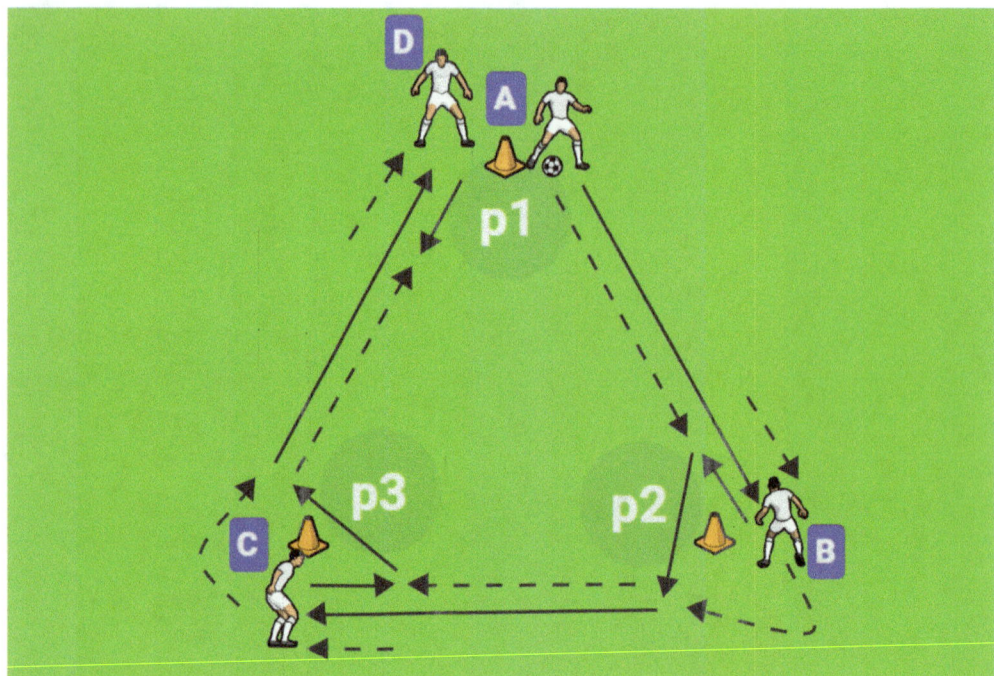

FIGURE 7.6D The triangle: one-two.

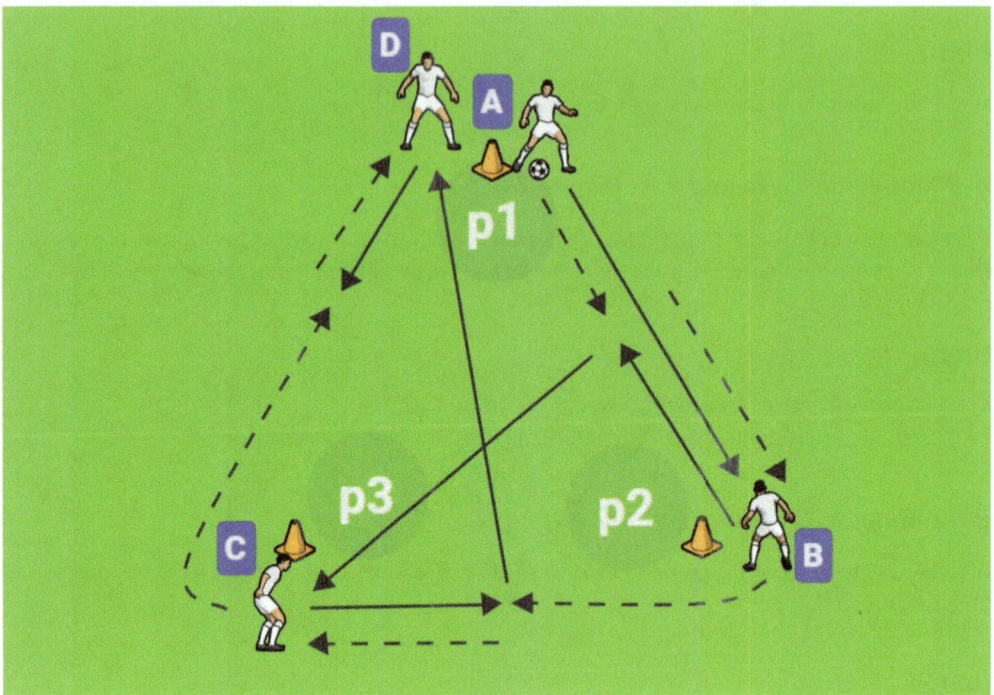

FIGURE 7.6E The triangle: diagonal.

12–15 Minutes: Diagonal (Figure 7.6e)

A to B to A to C to B (*A to P2*), B to D to C (*B to P3*), C to A (*C to P1*) and so on. One touch.

Hints:

- Players create space by moving away from the cone before receiving the ball.
- Players should receive and pass the ball with the outside leg.

Program 7: The Y

This program takes 15 minutes. It is a passing drill to develop the players' ability to make precise short passes; turn with the ball; and move to create space before receiving a pass. The receiving player should time movements to the pass and create space by first making a movement in the opposite direction (i.e., not stand and wait for the ball). Passes should be hard and along the grass, in front of the receiving player.

Preparation for: Tactical training, technical training, aerobic training and games.
Technical elements: Passing, turning with the ball and creating space.
Dimension: 40 m × 20 m per group.
Organization: Groups of 7 to 12 players.
Equipment: 2 balls and 4 cones per group.

0–3 Minutes: Passing

Each group moves freely on the pitch with two balls:

- Pass with one touch.
- Pass with obligatory two touches.

3–6 Minutes: Dynamic Stretching

Each group conducts various dynamic stretching exercises, each lasting 20 seconds. Players from each group alternate selecting the exercises (see page 67).

6–9 Minutes: One Touch (Figure 7.7a)

A to B to C to D to B to D to C (*A to P3; B to P4; C stays; D to P2*), C to A to E to F to A to F to E (*C to P3; A to P4; F to P1; E stays; A to P4; F to P1*) and so on. One touch.

9–12 Minutes: Turning (Figure 7.7b)

A to B to C to D to E (*A to P3; B to P4; C to P3; D to P3; E to P3*) and so on. One touch, except for turning (two touches).

Hints:

- When turning, first touch in the direction of the following pass.

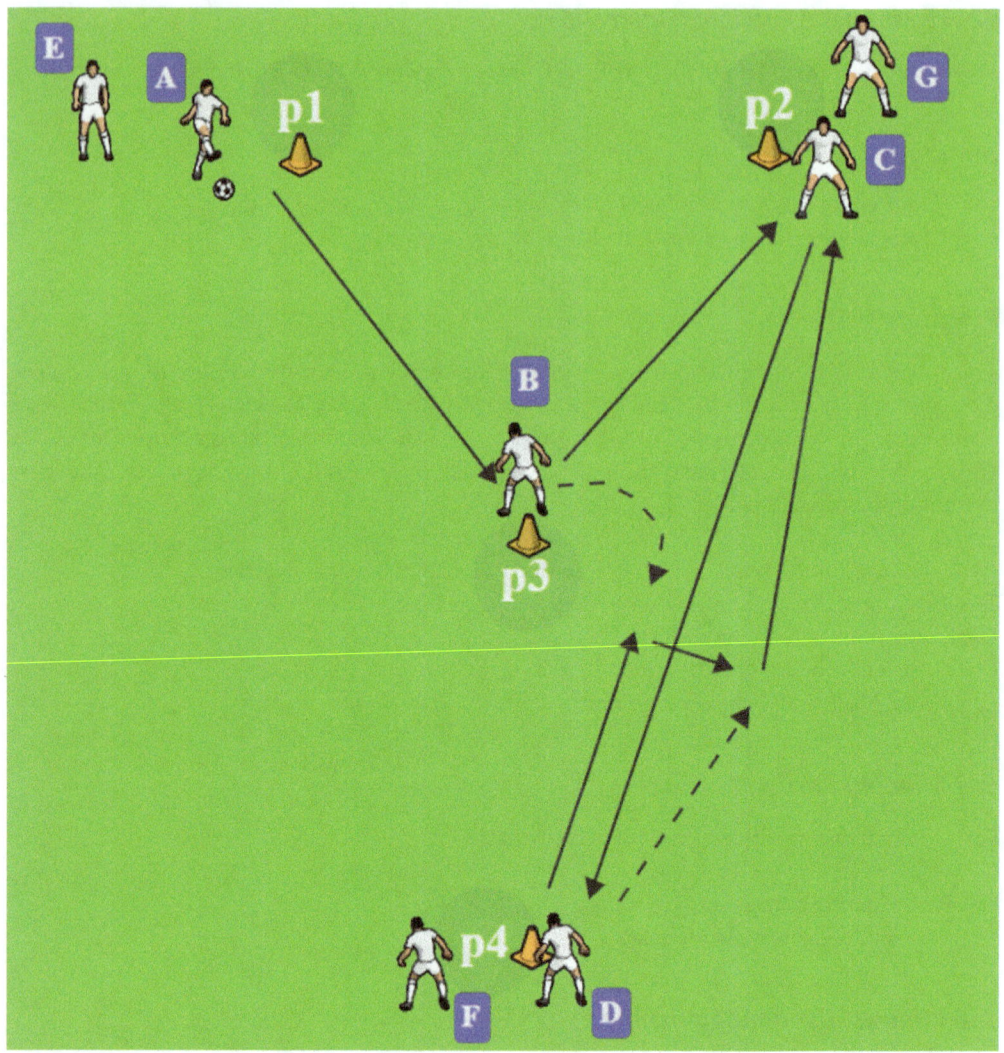

FIGURE 7.7A The Y: one touch.

12–15 Minutes: One-Two (Figure 7.7c)

A to B to A to C to B to C to D (*A to P3; B to P4; C to P2*), D to A to D to E to A to E to F (*D to P3; A to P4; E to P3*), and so on. One touch.

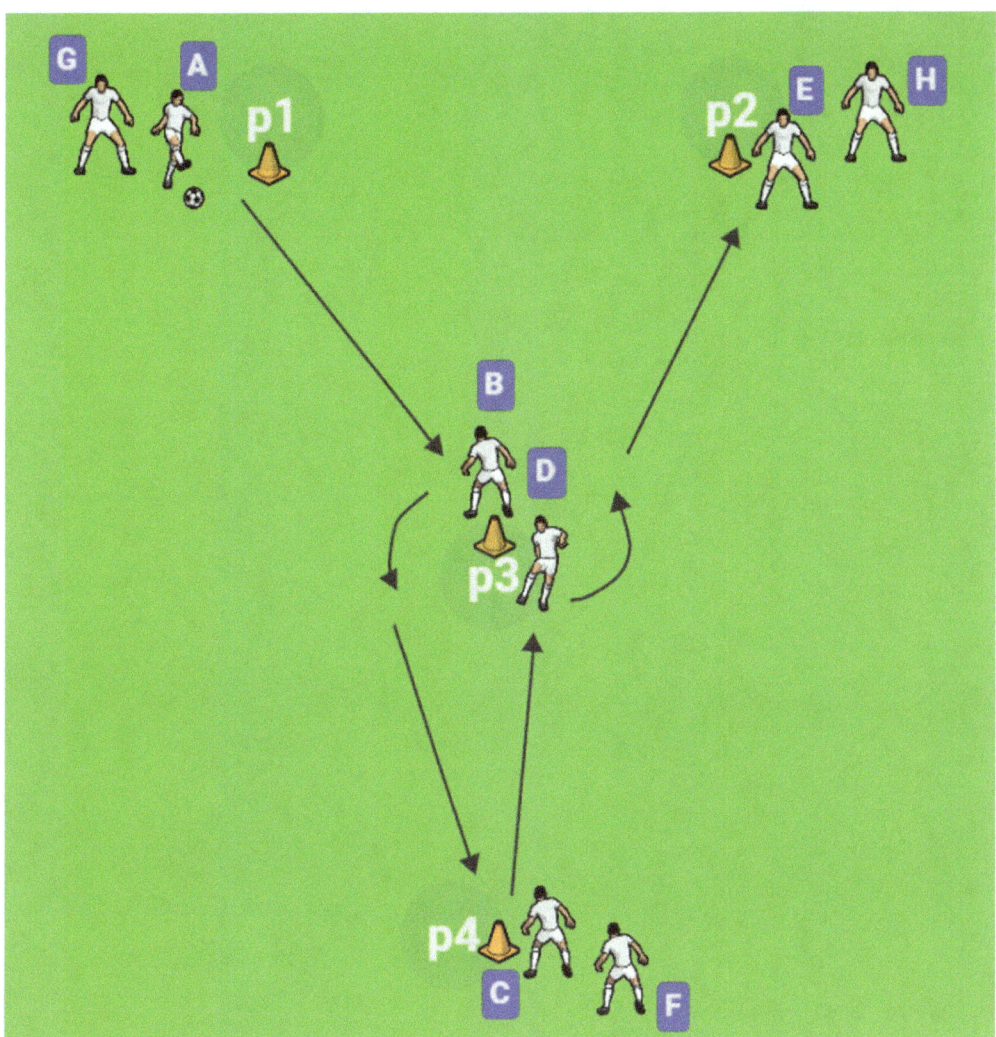

FIGURE 7.7B The Y: turning.

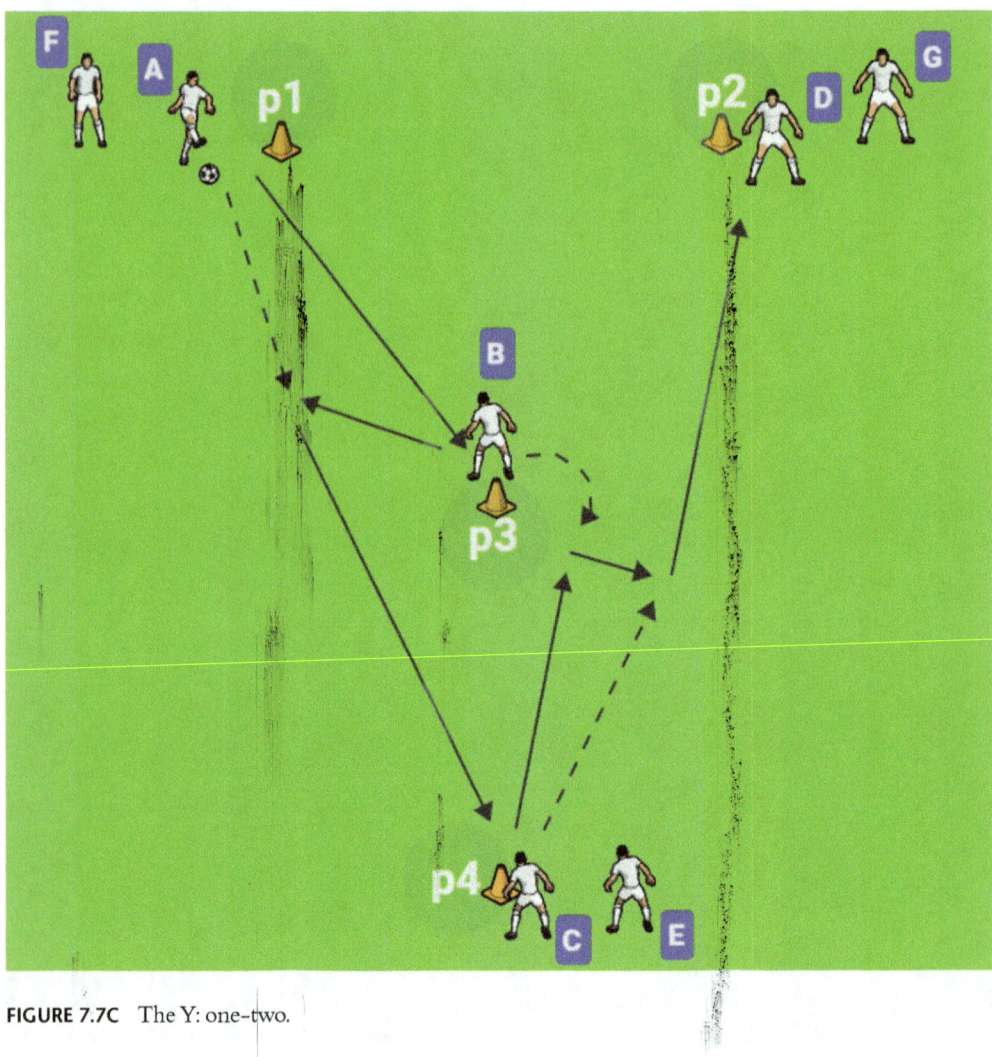

FIGURE 7.7C The Y: one-two.

Program 8: The Cross

This program lasts 15 minutes and consists of a passing drill to develop the players' ability to make and receive short-distance passes, as well as to create space and use correct timing of the movement before receiving the ball.

Preparation for: Tactical training, technical training, aerobic training and games.
Technical elements: Flat strong passes with the inside of the foot and controlling the ball when receiving.
Dimension: 20 m × 20 m per group.
Organization: Groups of 6 to 10 players.
Equipment: 2 balls and 5 cones per group.

0-3 Minutes: Activities and Jogging (Figure 7.8a)

Players are organized in four groups and positioned on the four outside cones of the "cross." Players do a dynamic stretching exercise while moving toward the center of the cross and jog back to the outside cone. Players from each group alternately select an exercise (see page 67) and move together.

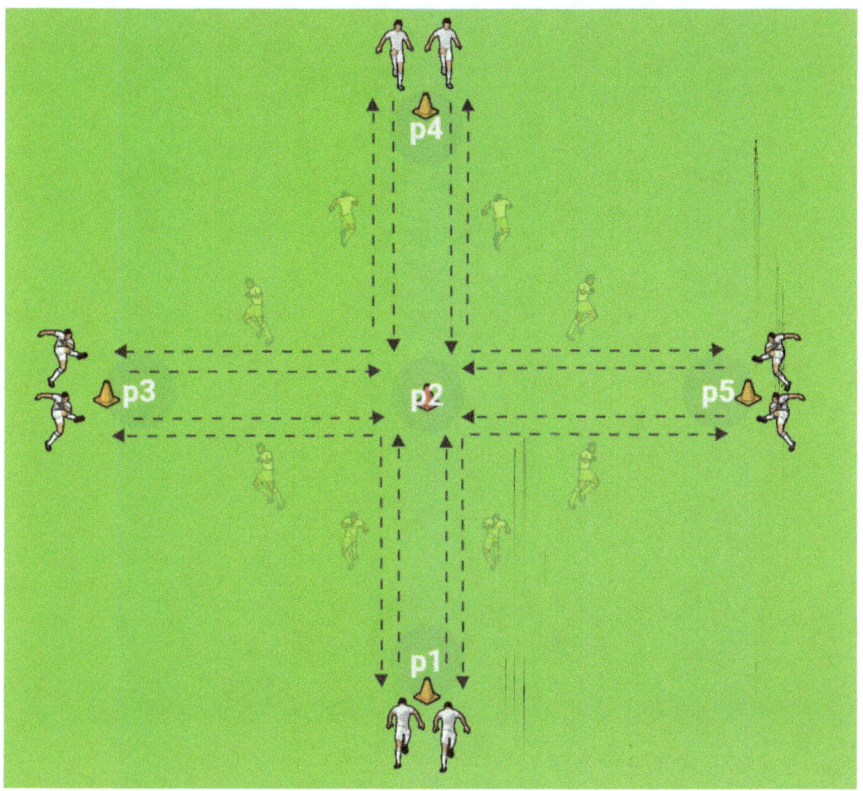

FIGURE 7.8A The cross: activities and jogging.

3–6 Minutes: Tiki-taka (Figure 7.8b)

A to B to A to C to A to B to D (*A to P2; C to P3; B to P4*). Two balls are played simultaneously from the bottom and the top of the cross. One touch. The direction of play changes after 90 seconds. Speed is gradually increased. This also applies to the next two drills.

6–9 Minutes: One-Two (Figure 7.8c)

A to B to A to C to A to C to D (*A to P2; C to P3; B to P4*). One touch.

9–12 Minutes: Between (Figure 7.8d)

A to B to A deep to C to D (*A to P2; C to P3; B to P4*). One touch.

12–15 Minutes: Various

Players choose from the previous three variations.

Hints:

- Players have to adhere to the offside line (the middle of the cross).
- Deep runs are performed with high speed during "tiki-taka"; near-maximum speed during "one-two"; and maximum speed during "between" and "various."

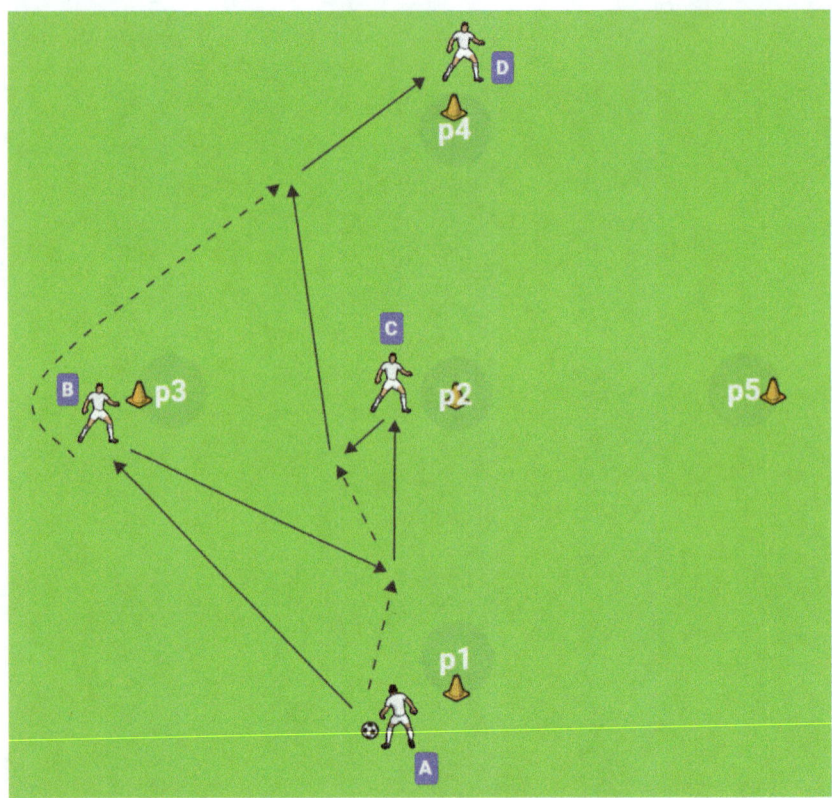

FIGURE 7.8B The cross: tiki-taka.

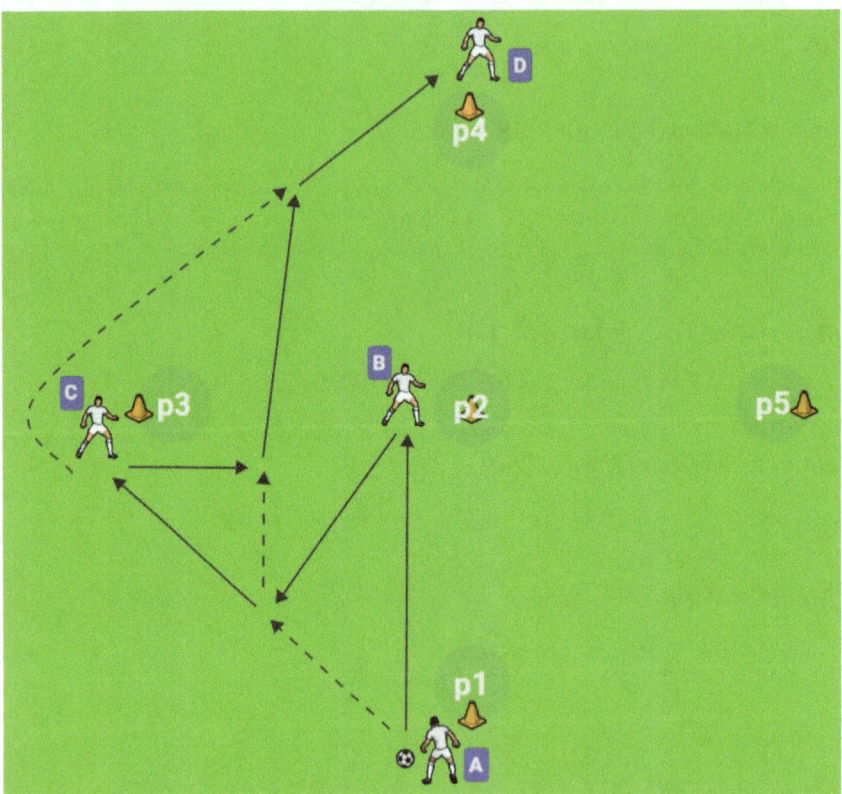

FIGURE 7.8C The cross: one-two.

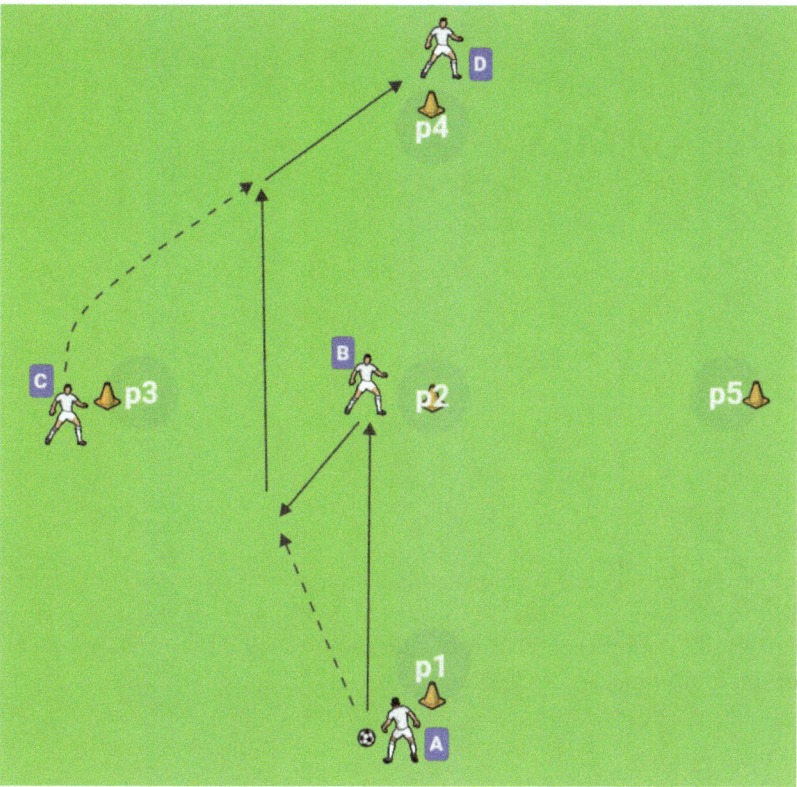

FIGURE 7.8D The cross: between.

Summary

Doing warm-ups with the ball has the great advantage that it also develops the players' technical and, for some drills, tactical skills. Furthermore, it is also motivating for the players.

8
WARM-UP GAMES

Small-sided games can be used to prepare the players for the following training. It should be emphasized that it is recommended that the player do 3–5 minutes of dynamic stretching and activities with the ball before starting playing. A number of games that can be used are presented here. The duration of the programs is 10–20 minutes.

Program 1: Phases

In this program, the players are doing small-sided games in phases focusing on accurate passes as well as creating space and moving in free space. Thus, fundamental technical and tactical elements are trained.

Preparation for: Tactical training, technical training, aerobic training, speed endurance training, speed and agility training.
Technical elements: Passing and stopping.
Tactical elements: Provide opportunities for the player with the ball and utilize free space.
Players: 24 (16–30) and 2 goalkeepers (in last phase).
Dimension: A full pitch divided into zones (see Figure 8.1a–c).
Organization: Pairs (i.e., 12 pairs [goalkeepers together], with a ball).
Equipment: 12 balls.

Hints for execution of the small-sided games:

- Three phases with gradually increased intensity.
- Coach primarily the tactical elements.
- Program can be shortened by excluding one or two of the three phases.
- Create passing opportunities for the player with the ball.
- Use high speed when changing zone.

0–3 Minutes: Passing

Pairs are passing, alternating between one and two touches.

3–5 Minutes: Dynamic Stretching

For exercises, see page 67.

5–10 Minutes: Playing 4 vs. 2 (Phase One)

Twenty-two zones (no play in gray zones; Figure 8.1a). Four *groups of 6 players*.

Playing 4 vs. 2 with two touches: If one of the two players touches the ball, the player changes with the player who made the mistake. A ball kicked out of the playing area is also a mistake. If the ball is played into another zone, all players have to move to this zone.

10–15 Minutes: Playing 3 vs. 3 (Phase Two)

Twelve zones (no play in gray zones; Figure 8.1b).

3 vs. 3 with free touch: 1 point is given with 10 consecutive passes without the opposing team touching the ball. The play can change zone, but all players need to enter the zone before going to another zone.

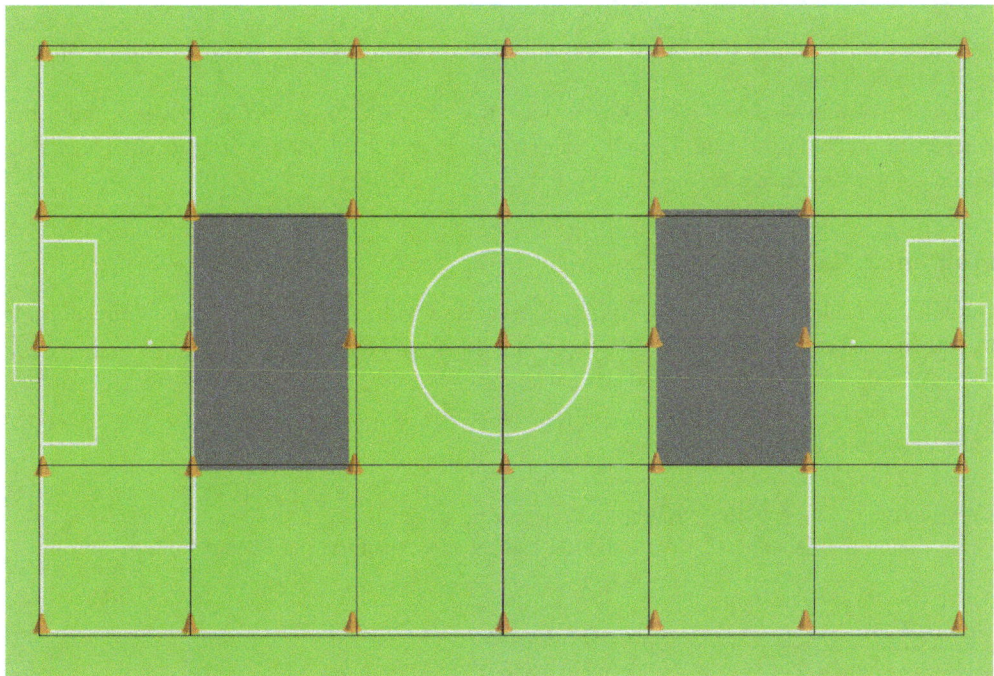

FIGURE 8.1A Phase one: 4 vs. 2.

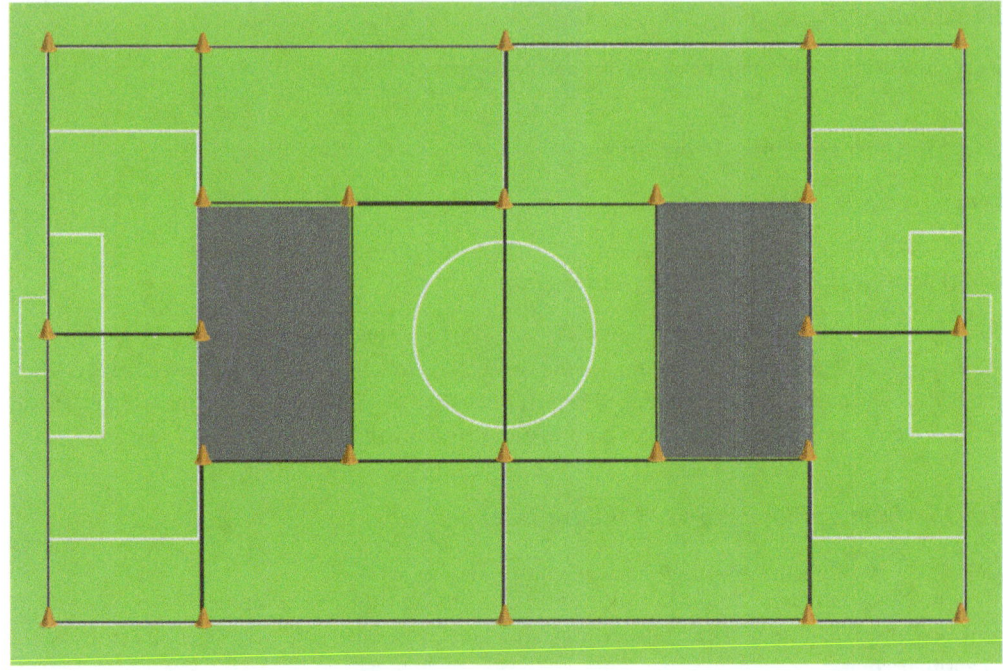

FIGURE 8.1B Phase two: 3 vs. 3.

15–20 Minutes: Playing 6 vs. 6 (Phase Three)

Two zones (see Figure 8.1c). Two groups of 12 players (plus 1 goalkeeper with each group that plays with both teams).

6 vs. 6 with a maximum of two touches: 1 point is given with 10 consecutive passes without the other team touching the ball. The play can change zone, but all players need to enter the zone before going to another zone.

Program 2: Catch

Catch is a fun and effective way of making players move with high speed in different directions. It may be selected at times where the players need to laugh and have fun.

Preparation for: Tactical training, technical training, aerobic training.
Technical elements: Passing and stopping.
Players: 12 (6–22).
Dimension: Half of a penalty area (Figure 8.2).
Organization: Two "catchers" (shirt in hand). Half of the remaining players (i.e., 5) have a ball.

Description

"Catchers" catch a player without a ball, who becomes the new "catcher."

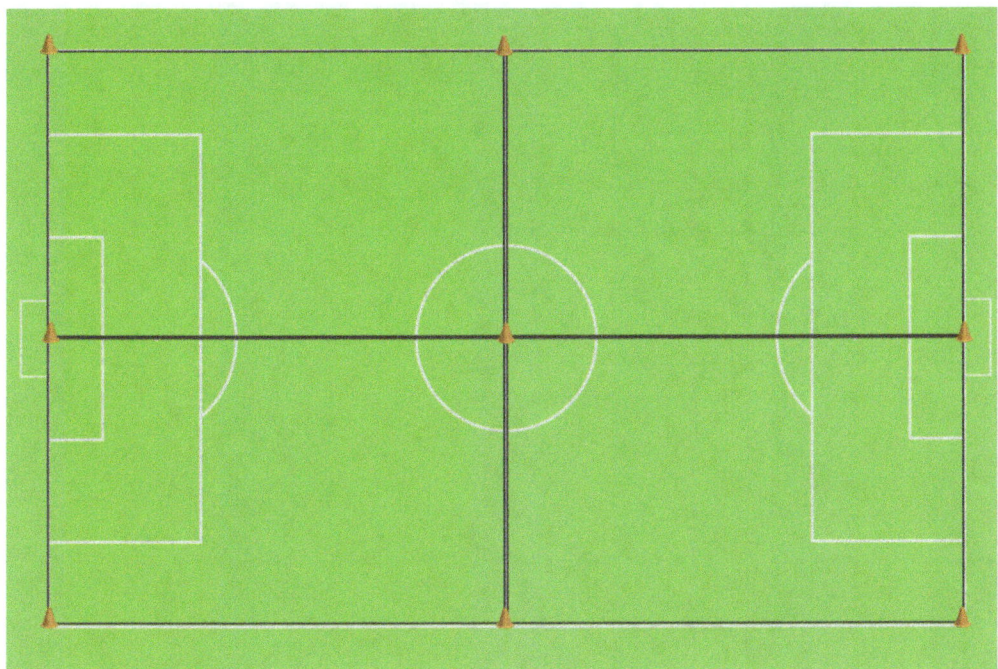

FIGURE 8.1C Phase three: 6 vs. 6.

Hints:

- Fun game.
- Players should pass to a "chased" player without being caught themselves.
- Balls out of area are recovered rapidly.
- Challenges internal relationships between the players (e.g., if a player stands with the ball, he/she does not contribute to the group).
- More players, more "catchers" and larger pitch (e.g., 20 players: 4 catchers, 8 balls and penalty area).
- Players hunting or being hunted work intensely. Demands among players may be quite different.

Variations:

1. Fewer balls.
   - Increase the loading of the players.
2. More "catchers."
   - Increase the loading of the players.
3. Ball out of the zone, player becomes "catcher."
   - Increase the precision of the passes.
   - More running of chased players.

FIGURE 8.2 Catch.

Program 3: Heading Ball

The focus is on moving in free space to receive the ball and make a competent header to score. It can be fun and can be used to break the normal warm-up routines, but it requires that all players are ready to fully contribute.

Preparation for: Tactical training, technical training, aerobic training.
Technical elements: Heading. Move the body to receive the ball in the right direction of play.
Tactical elements: Move to provide opportunities for the player with the ball.
Players: 12 (10–22).
Dimension: 25 m × 30 m (Figure 8.3).
Organization: Two teams (e.g., 5 vs. 5 plus 2 goalkeepers).
Equipment: 1 ball, 4 cones, 2 big or middle-sized goals.

Description

Play with the hands. Use a header to score.

- No steps with the ball.
- Maximum 3 seconds of possession.
- Change of possession if ball touches the ground.

Warm-Up Games **111**

FIGURE 8.3 Heading ball.

Hints:

- Fun game.
- Players should be encouraged to create space for each other.
- Players should move to create space to score.

Variations:

1. Every other ball has to be a header. Opponents cannot catch the ball when the ball is thrown.

    - Receiving player must focus on where to head before getting the ball.

2. A player with the ball can move 3 meters.

    - Makes it easier to pass and score.

3. Every other ball can be kicked in the air.

    - Requires more movements.

Program 4: Touch Football

Touch football can be exciting, as it requires a different way of thinking, since the attacking players have to be behind the ball at all times. Thus, it can be fun and develop the players' ability to handle new challenges.

FIGURE 8.4 Touch football.

Preparation for: Tactical training, technical training, aerobic training.
Technical elements: Dribbling and passing.
Tactical elements: Provide opportunities for the player with the ball. Utilize free space.
Players: 14 (10–22).
Dimension: One-third of a pitch (35 m × 65 m; Figure 8.4).
Organization: 2 teams (e.g., 7 vs. 7).
Equipment: 1 ball.

Description

No pass forward (like in rugby). Score by dribbling over the opponent's defending line.

- The other team gets the ball, if an opponent with the ball is touched on the back with the hand.
- The opposing team cannot intercept a pass.

Hints:

- Teammates to the player with the ball are placed behind the ball (throughout the width of the pitch).

Variations:

1. The opponent can intercept a pass.

    - Makes it more difficult for the attacking team. Introduced if it is too easy to score a goal.

2. A player can only dribble forward 20 meters or be in possession for 5 seconds.

    - If some players are very good and score often.
    - Not to decrease the intensity of other players.

3. The ball changes, when the opponent touches the ball.

    - Makes it more difficult for the attacking team.
    - Introduced if it is too easy to score a goal.

Program 5: Three Colors

The game aims at keeping possession when superior in numbers. It can be challenging, as the players need to keep track of which other team they can pass to, which develops their attention when having possession. The players' demands when "defending" can be quite high physically.

Preparation for: Tactical training, technical training, aerobic training, speed endurance training, speed and agility training.
Technical elements: Passing and stopping.
Tactical elements: Provide opportunities for the player with the ball. Utilize free space.
Players: 15 (9–21).
Dimension: About one-fourth of a pitch (30 m × 40 m; Figure 8.5).
Organization: 5 + 5 vs. 5 (three different colors).
Equipment: 1 ball.

Description

Two teams keep possession. The third team catches the ball.

- Maximum three touches.
- 10 passes without interception = 1 point.
- The team changes when the defending team recovers the ball.

Hints:

- Defending team members to collaborate to catch the ball.
- Possession teams to move to create passing opportunities.

Variations:

1. No pass to teammate.

    - More difficult.
    - Increase intensity and attention.

114 Warm-Up for Training and Testing

FIGURE 8.5 Three colors.

2. Maximum two touches.
   - More difficult.
   - Increase intensity.

3. Three first-time touches between three players in a row = 1 point.
   - More difficult.
   - Increase attention.
   - Fun.

Summary

Warm-up using games will stimulate the players and make them well prepared for most types of training. The games require technical and tactical skills of the players, and thereby they develop these skills.

9

WARM-UP FOR SPEED AND POWER TRAINING

Training with high power outputs, such as speed and power training, requires a special warm-up program. In this chapter, warm-ups for these types of training are discussed and programs are presented.

Warm-up for Speed Training

During speed training, the muscles are maximally engaged and high forces are applied to the joints. This creates a risk of injuries, and it is therefore important that the warm-up is specific, thorough and intense. Thus, the objective of the warm-up for speed training is to activate and increase the temperature in the muscles to be used, primarily calves, thighs, hip, glutes and core muscles. The program should include dynamic stretches, coordination exercise and footwork. To make the warm-up intense, the program also includes running with changes of speed and direction. If speed training is conducted with the ball, part of the warm-up should also be done with the ball.

A warm-up program follows that lasts about 15 minutes and is designed specifically for speed training without the ball. Warm-up programs for speed training with the ball can be found on pages 106 and 113.

In the first 10 minutes, the players are in the center circle. In the final 5 minutes, they are moving from side to side on the pitch.

0–2 Minutes: Static Stretching

Each stretch is performed for 2–3 seconds.

1. *Quads*: Bend one leg by grabbing just above the ankle, thereby standing on one leg. Reach opposite to the sky and move to the toes to introduce an element of balance. 10 repetitions.

2. *Hamstrings*: Keep one leg straight and placed in front of the other while keeping the back leg bent and the back straight. Move the hands toward the front foot to increase the stretch. 10 repetitions.

3. *Insides*: With one leg straight, take a step to the opposite side and bend the knee. Back is straight. 10 repetitions.

4. *Glutes*: While grabbing the ankle and the knee, pull the leg toward the chest to create a stretch of the gluteus and the outside of the thigh. 10 repetitions.

2–6 Minutes: Muscle Activation

5. *Handwalk*: From a standing position, reach the hands to the floor, and by small increments, move to a push-up position. Legs must be straight, and glutes and core muscles must be activated. Using small steps driven by the ankle, move the feet all the way to the hands. 3 repetitions.

6. *Sumo squat*: In a wide stance, reach a squat position with straight arms on the inside of the thighs and grab the toes. Next, look between the legs while at the same time stretching the legs as much as possible. Fingers grab the toes throughout. 5 repetitions.

7. *Step lunge*: Take a step back and drop into a lunge with the opposite arm going forward. From here, step into a forward lunge. Change sides and repeat. 5 times for each leg.

8. *Airplane*: Take a step forward while straightening the opposite arm. The hand in the air reaches for the toes of the front foot while the opposite leg is moved to a horizontal position. Change sides and repeat. 10 repetitions.

9. *Single-leg squat*: Squat as far down as possible without losing balance. Change legs and repeat. 10 repetitions.

10. *Squat jump*: From a standing position, drop down to a squat. From here, jump slightly forward. 10 repetitions.

11. *Jump with shoulder contact*: The players are together in pairs. Players perform a coordinated jump into the air and their shoulders contact. Players should now land on the ground and find their balance. 6 repetitions.

12. *Broad jumps*: From a standing position, jump as far as possible. Perform a countermovement with knees bent before takeoff and during landing. 3 jumps are performed in a row, with controlled landings in between, giving a transition phase of about 2 seconds. 5 repetitions.

6–10 Minutes: Dynamic Stretching

13. *Hip out*: Pull the knee toward the chest and move it to the side as far as possible; lower the leg, working the opposite abductor. 10 repetitions.

14. *Hip in*: Pull the knee out and up and move it in (while still in the air); lower the leg, working the opposite leg adductor. 10 repetitions.

Warm-Up for Speed and Power Training **121**

15. *Hamstring stretch*: Perform a forward kick, keeping the body straight with a straight leg and extended foot. Clapping under the knee will increase the stretch. 10 repetitions.

16. *Glutes*: Perform a forward kick with a twist while keeping the body straight. 10 repetitions.

17. *Leg extension stretch*: Pull the knee to the chest before the leg kicks out and down. 10 repetitions.

18. *Insides*: Keeping the body and leg straight, kick to the side. 10 repetitions.

122 Warm-Up for Training and Testing

19. *Hips*: Keeping the body and leg straight, kick the leg back and drive the opposite arm toward the back leg. 10 repetitions.

10–15 Minutes: Activities and Running

Two activities are carried out while moving from one side of the pitch to the other; on the way back, the player runs with progressively increased speed.

20. *Butt kicks*: Heels touch the glutes; arms move in the same motion as when running.

21. *High knees*: Move the knees to horizontal (one at a time).

22. *Skips*: Pull the knee to the chest and use the arms forcefully to contribute to each skip.

23. *Fast feet forward*: Make quick and short movements of the feet in a zig-zag pattern.

24. *Backward butt kicks*: Same as "butt kicks," but backward.

25. *Backward high knees*: Same as "high knees," but backward.

26. *Backward slalom*: Run backward in a slalom pattern; look over the shoulder to orientate.

27. *Fast feet backward*: Same as "fast feet forward," but backward; look over the shoulder to orientate.

28. *Sidesteps*: Move sideways with a low center of gravity; change sides every 3 steps.

29. *Carioca (moving left)*: Moving sideways, the right leg changes between stepping in front and back of the left. When in front, pull the knee up to a 90-degree angle at the beginning of the step and bring it down at the end.

30. *Carioca (moving right)*: Moving sideways, the left leg changes between stepping in front and back of the right. When in front, pull the knee up to 90-degree angle at the beginning of the step and bring it down at the end.

31. *Headers*: Perform jumps on right, left and both legs.

32. *Accelerations*: Accelerate forward 10 meters, turn and accelerate for 2 meters in the opposite direction, then turn and accelerate 10 meters.

33. *Decelerations*: Sprint forward 10 meters, decelerate and take 2–3 steps backward, then sprint forward 10 meters.

34. *Zorro sprints*: Sprint and plant in a Z-pattern (sprint and plant left, sprint and plant right) and in a mirrored Z (sprint and plant right, sprint and plant left); all runs are 3–5 meters.

35. *Backward and forward sprinting*: Sprint backward for 10 meters, turn and sprint forward 10 meters.

Warm-up for Power Training

The aim of warm-up for power training is to increase body temperature and to activate the muscles used during the power training. The external loading in power training applies more than usual stress to the muscles, ligaments and joints, which increases the risk of injury. It is therefore important that the warm-up prepares for situations where the muscles, ligaments and joints are vulnerable and where an injury can occur.

Basic warm-up exercises can include jogging, stair-climbing, rope skipping, ergometer cycling and rowing, which should be performed initially for a minimum of 5 minutes to generate a rise in body temperature. Then, specific muscle exercises are to be performed that increase the compliance, flexibility and "preparedness" of the muscles, ligaments and joints. These are performed for another 5 minutes; however, it depends on the power program (i.e., the number of muscles that are to be exercised). Often, power training is performed indoors, which may limit the available space for the warm-up, especially if the session is planned for the whole squad. Given next is an indoor warm-up program for power training for individuals and for a squad. The program lasts 15 minutes. If the power program is conducted on the pitch, the warm-up program on page 75 can be used.

0–5 Minutes: Basic Warm-up

Basic warm-up exercises may include jogging, stair-climbing, rowing, cycling, striding and rope skipping. Exercises are performed for 5 minutes to generate heat in the body, which will increase the compliance, flexibility and preparedness of the muscles, ligaments and joints.

5–15 Minutes: Specific Warm-up

1. *Combination stretch*: From a standing position, take a step forward with the right leg and put the left hand on the ground next to the right foot (shoulder-width apart). Place the right hand in between the legs and grab the outside of the ankle on the right foot; the inside will be stretched (the stretch will increase by twisting the torso to the left). Next, the right hand is placed to the right of the right foot (which is now in the middle of the two hands) and glutes move backward and toes on the right foot are lifted, which creates a stretch on the backside. Both arms are now lifted and the upper body becomes vertical to stretch the hip; turning the arms to the right will increase the stretch. During the whole stretch, the back leg is stretched as much as possible. The body is moved to the starting position and the stretch is repeated on the other side. 3 repetitions on each side.

2. *Sumo squat*: From a standing position, move the feet to a wide stance; move the body to a squat position with straight arms on the inside of the thighs, then grab the toes (high chest) while looking to the sky. Next, look between the legs while stretching the legs as much as possible. Fingers grab the toes throughout. 10 repetitions.

3. *Hand walk*: From a standing position, reach the hands to the floor, and by small increments, move as far forward as possible (without tumbling); legs must be straight, glutes and core muscles must be activated; by using small steps driven by the ankle, move the feet all the way to the hands (remember the straight legs). 6 repetitions.

4. *Air squat*: From a standing position with feet shoulder-width apart, keep a straight back with a high-lifted chest throughout the exercise. Squat down as far as possible. Bring the arms in front of the body to increase balance and stability. Return to the starting position by contracting the glutes fully and actively moving the arms. 15 repetitions.

5. *Squat jump*: Same as "air squat," but with a jump at the end. 10 repetitions.

6. *Lunge*: From a standing position, lift one knee toward the chest. Step out and move the body down toward the surface. The glutes move back toward the heel of the back leg and the weight is distributed on the heel of the front foot. Use the arms actively to increase balance and stability, and flex the elbows at a 90-degree angle. The front leg kicks the body back to the starting position and the opposite leg moves up and forward. 10 repetitions.

7. *Lunge jump*: Same as "lunge," but perform a jump and switch position of legs mid-air. 4 repetitions.

8. *Mountain climber:* Start in a plank position. Squeeze the glutes and pull the shoulders away from the ears. Pull the right knee to the chest, and then quickly push the right leg back while switching and pulling the left knee to the chest. Continue to switch knees using a running motion. Core stability is essential. 30 seconds.

9. *5–5–5:* 5 narrow push-ups, 5 normal-width push-ups and 5 wide push-ups.

10. *Front to back*: Start by standing upright. At the same time, move both feet front and back as fast as possible across an imaginary line. Use arms purposely in the direction of the movement. 10 seconds.

11. *Lateral*: Same as front to back, but moving the body laterally, like slalom skiing, across the imaginary line. The center of gravity should stay above the line. Move feet as fast as possible. Make sure not to rotate. 10 seconds.

12. *Switch*: One foot goes across the imaginary line together with the opposite arm. Then switch and move the other leg and arm across. Switch as fast as possible. 10 seconds.

 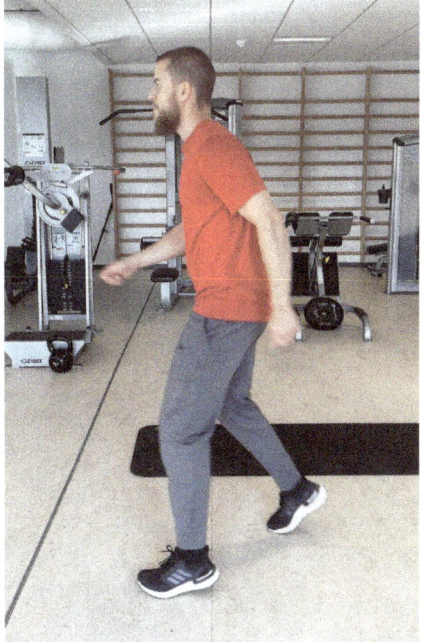

13. *High knees*: Start by standing upright. Move one knee at a time to a 90-degree angle. Elbows are locked at a 90-degree angle. The left arm comes forward when the right knee is in the air and vice versa. 10 seconds.

14. *Running in place*: Tap the floor as fast as possible. 10 seconds.

Summary

Training with high-power outputs, such as speed and power training, requires a specific warm-up that is thorough and intense to avoid injuries and optimize the effect of training. The focus of the warm-up for speed and power training is to increase body temperature and to activate the muscles used during training such as calves, thighs, hip, glutes and core muscles.

10
WARM-UP FOR TESTING

Warm-up can significantly affect test results. For example, jumping performance may be 15% better after a warm-up period that elevates the muscle temperature by about 3°C. Therefore, it is important to perform a proper and standardized warm-up before a test in order to obtain the best test result and to be able to compare with previous test results. This chapter provides specific warm-up programs for commonly used tests in football as described in Bangsbo and Mohr (2015).

Yo-Yo Intermittent Tests

See Bangsbo and Mohr (2015) for information on how to conduct the tests.

A thorough warm-up needs to be carried out before performing a Yo-Yo intermittent test at maximum (i.e., to exhaustion). The players have to be prepared for the high cardiovascular demands and the loading during the turns. Thus, it is important to ensure that the muscle and body temperature are elevated before the test and that the players have tried the turns prior to the test. The Yo-Yo intermittent endurance test is less intense at the beginning than the Yo-Yo intermittent recovery test, so the duration of the warm-up is shorter.

Yo-Yo Intermittent Endurance Test

0–2 minutes: Jogging.
2–4 minutes: Dynamic stretching.
4–6 minutes: Perform the first three levels of the test.
6–7 minutes: Dynamic stretching and preparing for the test.

Yo-Yo Intermittent Recovery Test

0–2 minutes: Jogging.
2–4 minutes: Dynamic stretching.
4–7 minutes: Intermittent running alternating between 30 seconds at moderate intensity and 30 seconds at low intensity.
7–9 minutes: Perform the first three levels of the test.

9–10 minutes: Dynamic stretching and preparing for the test.

Non-exhaustive Yo-Yo Intermittent Endurance Test and Yo-Yo Intermittent Recovery Test

The submaximum version of the Yo-Yo tests is used to evaluate the heart-rate response in the last phase of the test as well as in recovery after the test. The heart rate during the test is influenced by the work before the test; therefore, it is particularly important that the warm-up program and duration are standardized. As the first part of the test is performed at moderate speed, the warm-up is carried out for only 5 minutes and the intensity is low.

0–2 minutes: Jogging.
2–5 minutes: Dynamic stretching.

Sprint and Agility Tests

See Bangsbo and Mohr (2015) for information on how to conduct the tests.

Sprint and agility tests are to be performed with maximum effort and a thorough warm-up is necessary, particularly for the leg and hip muscles. Nonetheless, sprinting and agility are whole-body movements and core, arm and shoulder muscles should also be carefully warmed up.

The following are warm-up programs for specific sprint and agility tests.

The Linear Sprint Test

0–2 minutes: Jogging.
2–4 minutes: Dynamic stretching.
4–7 minutes: Alternating between 50-meter (about half a pitch) runs with progressive increasing speed and 50 meters jogging.
7–8 minutes: Dynamic stretching.
8–10 minutes: Perform the test at 80% and 90% of maximum speed separated by 1 minute.

The Curved Sprint Test

0–2 minutes: Jogging.
2–4 minutes: Dynamic stretching.
4–7 minutes: Alternating between 50-meter (about half a pitch) runs with progressive increasing speed and two 90-degree changes of direction, and 50 meters jogging.
7–8 minutes: Dynamic stretching.

8–10 minutes: Perform the test at 80% and 90% of maximum speed separated by 1 minute.

The Arrowhead Agility Test

0–2 minutes: Jogging.
2–4 minutes: Dynamic stretching.
4–7 minutes: Alternating between 50-meter (about half a pitch) runs with progressive increasing speed and two 90-degree changes of direction, and 50 meters jogging.
7–8 minutes: Dynamic stretching.
8–10 minutes: Perform the test at 80% and 90% of maximum speed separated by 1 minute.

The Creative Speed Test

0–2 minutes: Jogging.
2–4 minutes: Dynamic stretching.
4–7 minutes: Dribbling with change from low to moderate to high speed every 20 seconds; repeat three times for a total of 3 minutes.
7–8 minutes: Dynamic stretching.
8–10 minutes: Perform the test at 70% and 90% of maximum speed separated by 1 minute.

The Short Dribbling Test

0–2 minutes: Jogging.
2–4 minutes: Dynamic stretching.
4–7 minutes: Dribbling with change from low to moderate to high speed every 20 seconds; repeat three times for a total of 3 minutes.
7–8 minutes: Dynamic stretching.
8–10 minutes: Perform the test at 80% and 90% of maximum speed separated by 1 minute.

Jump Tests

See Bangsbo and Mohr (2015) for information on how to conduct the tests.

A jump test is used to test the power of a football player. Powerful movements, especially with maximum activation of the calves, thighs and glutes, create a need for a thorough warm-up of these muscles. The following program can be used both for the countermovement jump test and the five-jump test.

The Countermovement Jump Test and the Five-jump Test

0–2 minutes: Jogging.
2–4 minutes: Dynamic stretching.
4–6 minutes: Alternating between 50-meter (about half a pitch) runs with progressively increasing speed and 50 meters of jogging.
6–8 minutes: Five non-maximum (90% effort) jumps separated by 30 seconds of rest (i.e., 4 repetitions).
8–9 minutes: Dynamic stretching.
9–10 minutes: 2 maximum jumps separated by 1 minute.

Summary

Warm-up for testing needs to be standardized in order to ensure reliable and valid test results. This chapter provides clear guidelines for warm-ups for a number of relevant tests in football.

Bibliography

Bangsbo J, Mohr M. *Fitness testing in football.* www.soccerfitness.expert, 2015.

PART III
Match Preparation

Match preparation not only includes the traditional warm-up before a match but also the preparation just before the match, at halftime and before extra time, as well as warm-up for substitutes. It also includes optimizing performance using various procedures, such as using power exercises and garments.

11
WARM-UP FOR MATCH

Many years ago, one could see English teams go straight from the changing room to the pitch and start the match. Nowadays, every team understands that a proper warm-up is needed to optimize performance for the start of a match. However, a specific concern regarding warm-up for a match is that the players are doing too much, which will lead to depletion of their muscle carbohydrate (glycogen) stores and fatigue toward the end of the match (see Bangsbo 2017). In a survey of the 2010/11 English Premier League and Championship coaches, of whom 43% responded, the average warm-up time was 31 minutes, with a range of 15–45 minutes. About 90% of the clubs had a warm-up longer than 25 minutes. This is in contrast to a study demonstrating that a 12- to 16-minute warm-up program produced better performance than a 22- to 23-minute program, with both programs including small-sided games. It should be emphasized, however, that it is not the duration of the warm-up that is the problem, as low-intensity activities do not have a major impact on the muscle glycogen levels. It is rather the intense activities that are problematic. In particular, the sprints in the warm-up are demanding and have a great influence on muscle glycogen levels. Therefore, the number of sprints should be restricted.

Many players follow a warm-up routine they have developed over years and that makes them feel mentally prepared for the match. However, in many cases the warm-up is too demanding and actually reduces players' performance in the match. It is useful to film the players and later discuss the single elements with each player in order to optimize the warm-up. Most players like having some time by themselves with the coach to discuss their specific needs. An important element of the warm-up before a match is that the players work with the ball, not only to get a "feel" for the ball prior to the match but also to improve performance. Thus, sport-specific warm-ups, including small-sided games, have provided benefits over a general warm-up program by priming neural pathways and increasing neuromuscular activation (see Chapter 2).

The length of the warm-up may be restricted, and the period between the warm-up and the start of the match may be long due to various regulations often determined by commercial issues (e.g., television rights). If this is the case, the warm-up has to be tailored to match such criteria. Also, other factors (e.g., national anthem or photographing) may cause a long period between the warm-up and the match. In this case, it is of benefit to "keep warm" in the changing room using continued movements or heating garments. Ways to keep warm in the final period before the match are described in this chapter.

146 Match Preparation

Two programs that have a focus on both physical and technical preparation for the match are also presented in this chapter. The duration of each program is 20 minutes, with only short periods of intense activities in order to limit the muscle glycogen usage. For both programs, it is important that the players know the specific movements and drills, as unknown activities on a match day should be avoided.

Program 1: Team Warm-up

The warm-up starts with 5 minutes of activities and running to get to know the surface of the pitch, to increase muscle and body temperature and to activate the neuromuscular system (i.e., brain and muscles) with football-specific activities. Next, the players perform another 5 minutes of dynamic stretches to further activate and stretch key muscles. This period will prepare the muscles used in football in an energy-efficient way, as the heart rate is low. Next, a 5 vs. 5 possession game is played for 3 periods of 1 minute with 30 seconds of rest in between. Then the players do individual movements with and without the ball for 3 minutes. At the end, the players perform 2–3 sprints to ensure that they have fully engaged their neuromuscular system to match the demands of match play.

0–5 Minutes: Activities and Running

The players spend the first 5 minutes on activities and running for a distance of 40 meters (corresponding to the width of the penalty area). Activities are performed for half the course, while running is performed for the other half and so on. (see Figure 11.1).

FIGURE 11.1 The players alternate between one activity (half the course) and running (the other half of the course) for a total distance of 40 meters (corresponding to the width of the penalty area).

1. *Butt kicks*: Heels touch the glutes; arms move in the same motion as when running.

2. *High knees*: Move knees to horizontal (one at a time).

148   Match Preparation

3. *Skips*: Pull knee to the chest; use arms actively to contribute to each skip.

4. *Fast feet forward*: Make quick and short foot movements.

5. *Fast feet backward*: Make quick and short foot movements; look over the shoulder to orientate.

6. *Backward butt kicks*: Same as "butt kicks," but backward.

7. *Backward high knees*: Same as "high knees," but backward.

8. *Backward slalom*: Run backward while slaloming; look over the shoulder to orientate.

9. *Sidesteps*: Move sideways with a low center of gravity. Change sides after 3–4 steps.

5–10 Minutes: Dynamic Stretching

10. *Hip out*: Lift the knee to horizontal, move it to the side as far as possible and then lower it. 5 repetitions with each leg.

11. *Hip in*: Move knee out and up to horizontal, then move it in (while still in the air) and then down. 5 repetitions with each leg.

12. *Forward kick*: While keeping the body vertical, perform a straight-leg forward kick with extended foot. Clapping under the knee will increase range of movement. 5 repetitions with each leg.

13. *Forward kick with a twist*: While keeping the body vertical, perform a straight-leg forward kick with a twist in the hip. 5 repetitions with each leg.

14. *Leg extension stretch*: Lift knee to the chest, then extend the leg forward and down. 5 repetitions with each leg.

15. *Lateral kick*: Keep leg straight; move it to the side with the body kept straight. 5 repetitions with each leg.

16. *Hips*: Keeping the body and leg straight, kick the leg back and drive the opposite arm back toward the back leg. 5 repetitions with each leg.

17. *Air squat*: Squat down as far as possible with arms in front of the body to increase balance and stability. Return to the starting position by contracting the glutes fully and actively moving the arms. Keep a straight back with a high-lifted chest throughout the exercise. 5 repetitions.

18. *Squat jump*: Same as "air squat," but with a jump at the end. 3 repetitions.

154 Match Preparation

19. *Lunge*: Lift one knee toward the chest and step out, moving the body down toward the ground. The glutes are directed toward the heel of the back leg and the weight is distributed on the heel of the front foot. Use the arms actively to increase balance and stability, flexing elbows at a 90-degree angle. The front leg kicks the body back to the starting position and the opposite leg moves up and forward. 3 repetitions with each leg.

20. *Lunge jump*: Same as "lunge," but perform a jump and switch position of legs mid-air. 4 repetitions.

10–15 Minutes: Possession Game

A 5 vs. 5 game on a 25 m × 15 m pitch with 1 "wall" player (one touch) at each end (two of the substitutes). Game is played as 3 × 1 minute separated by 30 seconds of rest.

- In the first period, the players should become familiarized with how the ball acts on the pitch and when moving between teammates and opponents.
- In the second period, there is a maximum of two touches and the intensity of the game is increased.
- In the third period, there is still a maximum of two touches.

15–18 Minutes: Specific Movements With Ball

- Defenders may do headers and long balls.
- Central midfield players can do short and long passes.
- Attackers may shoot on goal with goalkeeper.
- Defenders and external midfield players can do crosses.

18–20 Minutes: Sprinting

- 2–3 15-meter sprints separated by 30 seconds of jogging.
- The sprints are performed in pairs to motivate the players to give maximum effort.

Program 2: Position-specific Warm-up

The overall aim of this warm-up program is to prepare the players in a position-specific manner. Often there is a restricted area available (less than half the pitch), but if incorporating the goalkeeper in the activities, the penalty area can also be used.

0–5 Minutes: Dynamic Stretching

The warm-up starts with dynamic stretching, where the players select exercises (see page 67) that suit their specific needs.

5–10 Minutes: Position-specific Exercises With the Ball

The players perform position-specific exercises with the ball. Central defenders may do headers and long passes. Central midfield players may receive and pass the ball in different positions. Defenders and external midfield players may make crosses. Attackers may receive the ball and lay it off and may also do headers.

10–15 Minutes: Attacking Drills

The team is organized from the midline toward the goalkeeper. Players are divided into a left-side and a right-side group, each consisting of two defenders, two midfield players and one offensive midfield player/attacker. The players pass to each other while moving forward to reach the goal as shown in Figure 11.2. The drill is carried out one side at a time. The players move back into position when the other group is active. The last period of the execution of the drill should include some maximum efforts including sprints, jumping and shots.

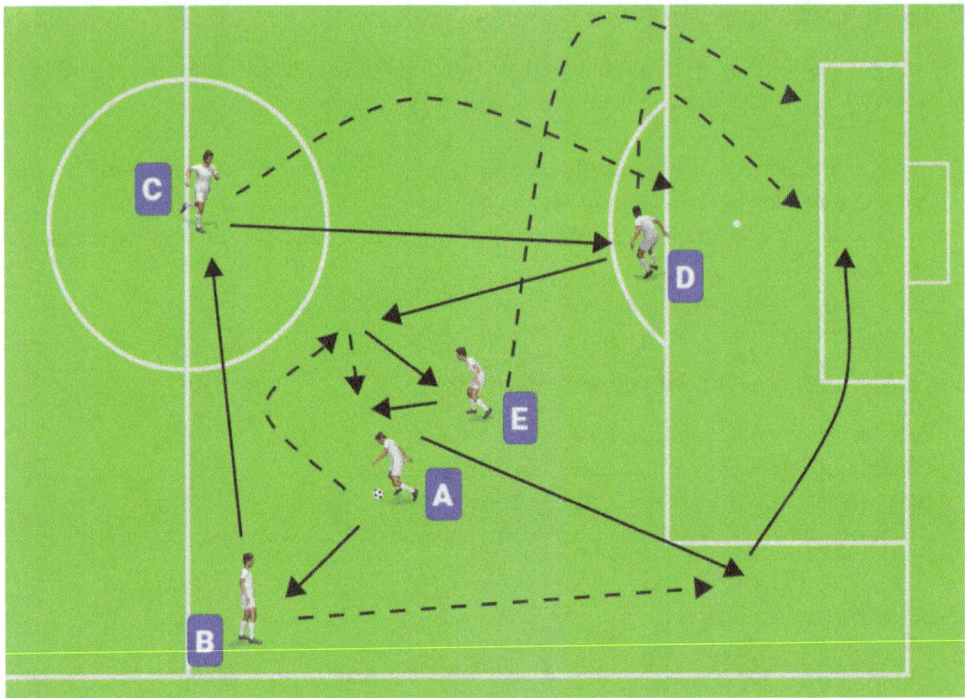

FIGURE 11.2 A passing drill for the whole team. Players are divided in two groups (right and left side) consisting of two defenders, two midfield players and one offensive midfield player/attacker. The ball is played from A to B to C to D to A to E to A to B who makes a cross to finish on goal for either D, E or C. The drill is carried out one side at a time. The players move back into position when the other group is active.

Warm-up in the Last Phase Before the Match

The warm-up before a match should continue until the start of the match. However, for professional players, it is a challenge that the warm-up often has to finish 15–20 minutes before kickoff due to regulations. This means that the body temperature of the players will decrease markedly before the match, and the muscle temperature will be back to resting level if the players are not doing any activities between the warm-up on the pitch and the match.

In European matches and some leagues, the players have to gather with the opponent team about 8 minutes before the match and line up together on the pitch about 2 minutes before kick-off. In these instances, it is important that the players are active in the changing room (after the warm-up on the pitch) before gathering with the other players, and also during the last 2 minutes on the pitch before kickoff. It should be stressed that not all activities are recommended, as accelerated depletion of muscle glycogen and early fatigue during the match can be a negative result of activities that are too intense.

The following are examples of activities that may be performed during the two periods. It should also be emphasized that it is important that the players drink during the warm-up and just before the match to avoid dehydration (see Bangsbo 2017).

Warm-Up for Match **157**

Program 3: Activities Conducted in the Changing Room Before the Players Gather for the Match

Exercises are performed for 20–30 seconds, with 20–30 seconds of rest in between. The program lasts 3–4 minutes, leaving time for the players to do their final preparations.

1. *Hip raise*: Lie flat on the back and move the feet to the butt. From this position, raise the hip and squeeze the glutes. Hold for 2 seconds at the top. 5 repetitions.

2. *Walk out push-ups*: From a standing position, move the hands to the floor while keeping the legs straight. Walk the hands out until a push-up position is reached. Do push-ups from this position. 5 repetitions.

   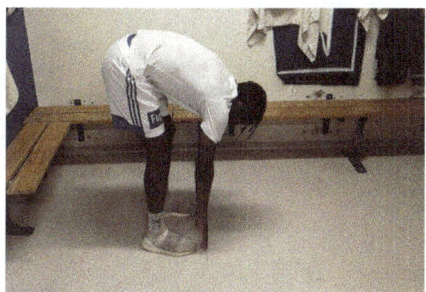 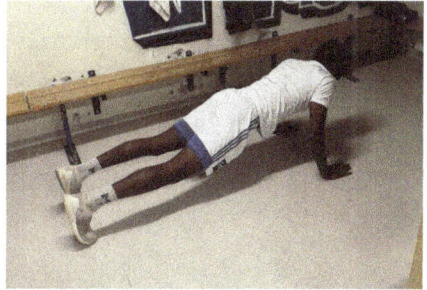

3. *Air squat*: From a standing position, squat down as far as possible. Hold the arms in front of the body to keep balance. 10 repetitions.

158 Match Preparation

4. *U back-lift*: Lie face down and lift arms and legs simultaneously. Hold for 2 seconds at the top. 10 repetitions.

Program 4: Activities Performed on the Pitch Right Before Kickoff

Run in repeated zig-zags with high intensity (not sprinting, as too much muscle glycogen will be used) for 5 seconds.

Various activities are performed for 15 seconds between the runs:

1. *Backward running*: Keep a steady pace.

2. *Sidesteps*: Keep a low center of gravity; change sides after 3 steps.

3. *High knees*: Make active use of the arms and lift the knees to horizontal.

4. *Skips*: Use the arms actively to assist in every skip.

Garments

An alternative or supplement to the activities conducted between the warm-up and the match is wearing garments that reduce a marked decrease in muscle temperature. In recent years, heated athletic garments (e.g., Adidas Clima365 and Blizzard survival jackets) have been developed and have been shown to be useful. Thus, wearing a Blizzard survival jacket during a 15-minute transition phase after a warm-up reduced the decrease in muscle temperature (from 0.55°C to 0.19°C) and led to better mean, fastest and total sprint time during a repeated sprint test in elite rugby players (see Figure 11.3).

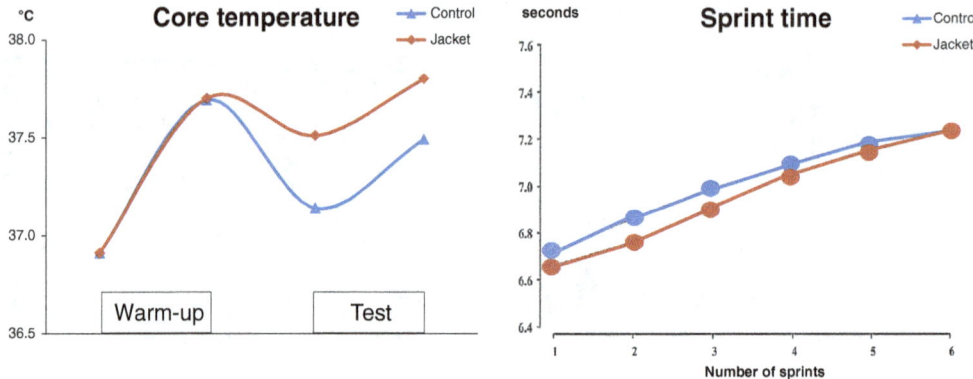

FIGURE 11.3 Core temperature (left) and time to complete a repeated sprint test (right) for players wearing a Blizzard survival jacket (red) or not (blue) during a 15-minute recovery phase after a warm-up.

Cooling During Warm-up in a Hot Environment

There may be some benefits to cooling the upper body during and after the warm-up. A group of male cyclists took part in a study where they were wearing head and neck ice wraps and an ice vest during a 20-minute warm-up period before completing a 16 km time trial in a hot environment (35°C and 44% relative humidity). Performance was compared to another occasion with the same warm-up and environment but with no cooling. It was observed that in the cooling situation, time to complete the 16 km time trial was 1 minute better than the no-cooling condition (29.3 vs. 30.3 minutes). Furthermore, the mean skin and body temperature as well as the rating of thermal comfort was higher in the cooling than in the no-cooling condition. To what extent wearing a cooling vest during warm-up in a hot environment can be applied in football is not clear, but the players may benefit from carrying the vest between the warm-up and the start of the match.

Re-warm-up at Halftime Is Not Used

When re-warm-up was introduced at halftime with the Juventus FC first team in 2001, the players went on the pitch after about 7 minutes of halftime. The spectators and journalists were very surprised and confused. However, they soon realized that this was part of an optimal preparation for the second half. Since then, very few teams are using this obvious strategy. It is probably for conservative reasons and lack of knowledge that few teams are utilizing the opportunity to prepare for the second half. It was proposed in the book *Fitness Training in Soccer: A Scientific Approach*, which was published in 1994 even before there was scientific evidence for the effects of the re-warm-up. But it does not appear to be lack of knowledge at an elite level, at least not in England. In a survey distributed to English Premier League and Championship practitioners, of whom 43% responded, 89% recognized the physiological benefits of re-warm-up at halftime. About two-thirds encouraged the players to do activities before the second half, but "unwillingness of the coach" and a "lack of time" were major constraints. They had on average 2.5 minutes for the re-warm-up. Factors such as match regulations, league policy and stadium facilities were not considered major barriers. Some coaches may say that they need all the time to provide tactical information to the players, but these may be given early at halftime, and they have to be short and precise anyway, so there should be enough time to do a proper re-warm-up.

Post-activation Potentiation

Muscular performance has been shown to be enhanced when preceded by maximal or near-maximal neuromuscular activation exercises. This phenomenon is termed post-activation potentiation (PAP). The use of a proper exercise preload to elicit a PAP response is a method that can be used before a match to increase the level of performance of the players, especially in the first period of the match and eventually also at the start of the second half.

Resistance exercises are typically used to induce the PAP response and have been demonstrated to increase performance in short-duration tasks, such as sprinting and jumping. For example, one study demonstrated that 2 × 5 deadlifts enhanced peak power output during the first 10 seconds of a 30-second sprint completed 10 minutes after the preload. In another study, the time to maximum velocity was shorter and peak power was higher in a 6-second sprint when preceded by 17 minutes of moderate intensity exercise and 4 × 4 (separated by 120 seconds of rest) maximum pedal revolutions against heavy resistance 4 minutes before the sprint. Also, enhanced peak power output (2%–5%) has been reported with drop jumps and weighted jumps as preload activities.

A number of factors may influence a player's ability to elicit a PAP response, and these include strength level and experience with power training, timing between the preload and subsequent muscle performance, and intensity and volume of the preload. Nevertheless, to elicit a positive PAP response, power exercises at moderate intensity (60%–85% 1RM) should be selected both for players who are inexperienced or experienced with power training. Inexperienced players should do only one set, while experienced players should do multiple sets. Top-class players may benefit from lifting heavier loads of up to 95% 1RM.

It should be noted that some studies have reported no improvement or even a negative impact on performance following a preload, which may have been caused by fatigue since mechanisms of muscle potentiation and fatigue coexist, and any performance benefits depend on the balance between these two factors.

Improvements in power output do occur after 5–20 minutes, but in experienced individuals, transition duration of about 10 minutes seems to be optimal. Ideally, each player should find the optimal load in exercises that engage a large muscle mass such as squats, deadlifts and hip thrusts, as well as an optimal transition duration to maximize their power-generating capabilities in a match.

Some guidelines for a preload program follow that will elicit a PAP response, including exercises such as deadlifts, squats, hip thrusts, Olympic lifts, or ballistic-style preloading activities such as drop jumps and weighted jumps (see Bangsbo 2013).

Level	Inexperienced	Experienced	Elite
Load	60%–85% 1RM	60%–85% 1RM	Up to 95% 1RM
Sets	One	Multiple	Multiple
Reps	Few	Few	Few
Transition duration	<10 min	~10 min	~10 min

Summary

Warm-up for a match is essential for performance in the match, but often the warm-up is too long and too intense, causing a negative effect on performance at the start and toward the end of the match. A warm-up lasting 10–15 minutes is suitable, but it can be longer if the additional time is spent on low-intensity activities. Including specific preload exercises in the warm-up, such as squats or drop jumps, can be beneficial for power-generating capabilities in the match. However, the impact of different variables will vary among players, and it is therefore advised to tailor the preload to the individual player.

In elite football, where the break between the warm-up and the match may be up to 20 minutes, the players should be active in this period and wear garments for passive heat maintenance.

Warm-ups should also be conducted in a hot environment, but the players may benefit from cooling the upper body before the match.

Bibliography

Bangsbo J. *Nutrition in football.* www.soccerfitness.expert, 2017.

Bangsbo J. *Power training in football.* www.soccerfitness.expert, 2013.

Clark RA, Bryant AL, Reaburn P. The acute effects of a single set of contrast preloading on a loaded countermovement jump training session. *The Journal of Strength & Conditioning Research* 20: 162–166, 2006.

Docherty D, Hodgson MJ. The application of postactivation potentiation to elite sport. *International Journal of Sports Physiology and Performance* 2: 439–444, 2007.

Gabbett TJ, Sheppard JM, Pritchard-Peschek KR, Leveritt MD, Aldred MJ. Influence of closed skill and open skill warm-ups on the performance of speed, change of direction speed, vertical jump, and reactive agility in team sport athletes. *The Journal of Strength & Conditioning Research* 22: 1413–1415, 2008.

Katica CP, Wingo JE, Herron RL, Ryan GA, Bishop SH, Richardson M. Impact of upper body precooling during warm-up on subsequent time trial paced cycling in the heat. *Journal of Science and Medicine in Sport* 21: 621–625, 2018.

Kilduff LP, Bevan HR, Kingsley MI, Owen NJ, Bennett MA, Bunce PJ, Hore AM, Maw JR, Cunningham DJ. Postactivation potentiation in professional rugby players: optimal recovery. *The Journal of Strength & Conditioning Research* 21: 1134–1138, 2007.

Kilduff LP, Finn CV, Baker JS, Cook CJ, West DJ. Preconditioning strategies to enhance physical performance on the day of competition. *International Journal of Sports Physiology and Performance* 8: 677–681, 2013.

Kilduff LP, Owen N, Bevan H, Bennett M, Kingsley MI, Cunningham D. Influence of recovery time on post-activation potentiation in professional rugby players. *Journal of Sports Sciences* 26: 795–802, 2008.

Russell M, Tucker R, Cook CJ, Giroud T, Kilduff LP. A comparison of different heat maintenance methods implemented during a simulated half-time period in professional rugby union players. *Journal of Science and Medicine in Sport* 21: 327–332, 2018.

Russell M, West DJ, Briggs MA, Bracken RM, Cook CJ, Giroud T, Gill N, Kilduff LP. A passive heat maintenance strategy implemented during a simulated half-time improves lower body power output and repeated sprint ability in professional rugby union players. *PLoS One* 18, 10: e0119374, 2015.

Sale D. Postactivation potentiation: role in performance. *British Journal of Sports Medicine* 38: 386–387, 2004.

Scott SL, Docherty D. Acute effects of heavy preloading on vertical and horizontal jump performance. *The Journal of Strength & Conditioning Research* 18: 201–205, 2004.

Thatcher R, Gifford R, Howatson G. The influence of recovery duration after heavy resistance exercise on sprint cycling performance. *The Journal of Strength & Conditioning Research* 26: 3089–3094, 2012.

Tillin MNA, Bishop D. Factors modulating post-activation potentiation and its effect on performance of subsequent explosive activities. *Sports Medicine* 39: 147–166, 2009.

Turner AP, Bellhouse S, Kilduff LP, Russell M. Postactivation potentiation of sprint acceleration performance using plyometric exercise. *The Journal of Strength & Conditioning Research* 29, 2: 343–350, 2015.

Ugrinowitsch C. Meta-analysis of postactivation potentiation and power: effects of conditioning activity, volume, gender, rest periods, and training status. *The Journal of Strength & Conditioning Research* 27: 854–859, 2013.

West DJ, Russell M, Bracken RM, Cook CJ, Giroud T, Kilduff LP. Post-warmup strategies to maintain body temperature and physical performance in professional rugby union players. *Journal of Sports Sciences* 34: 110–115, 2016.

Wilson JM, Duncan NM, Marin PJ, Brown LE, Loenneke JP, Wilson SMC, Jo E, Lowery RP, Ugrinowitsch C. Meta-analysis of postactivation potentiation and power: effects of conditioning activity, volume, gender, rest periods, and training status. *The Journal of Strength & Conditioning Research* 27, 3: 854–859, 2013.

12
RE-WARM-UP AT HALFTIME AND BEFORE EXTRA TIME

Running distance in the beginning of the second half is markedly shorter than the beginning of the first half (see Figure 12.1). In addition, it has been observed that as much as 20% of elite football players have their least intense 15-minute period in a match during the initial part of the second half. This is remarkable, considering that the players at halftime had 15 minutes to recover. One possible explanation is the lack of physical preparation for the second half. Body temperature, and muscle temperature in particular, does decrease significantly during halftime (see Figure 12.2). Furthermore, scientific studies have demonstrated that the sprinting and jumping ability of players is reduced at the start of the second half compared with the end of the first half (see Figures 12.3 and 12.4). Considering that players' ability to make explosive actions, such as sprints and jumps, can be crucial for the outcome of the match, it is valuable to physically prepare players for the second half.

In order to avoid the decrease in muscle temperature, the players should perform some activities at halftime and do a short (5–7 minutes) re-warm-up program consisting of low- and moderate-intensity exercise before the second half, especially when the break lasts more than 10 minutes. When a group of players followed such a procedure, they regained muscle and body temperature (see Figure 12.5), and they had the same sprinting capacity at the start of the second half as before the match (see Figure 12.3). Also, most of the jumping capacity could be regained (see Figure 12.4). It also had a positive effect on the cardiovascular system. Thus, the heart rate rose more rapidly at the start of the second half when activities were done at halftime in a simulated match compared to passive recovery (see Figure 12.6). It has also been shown that a 5RM leg-press re-warm-up after a 26-minute period of intermittent activities improved rate of force development and repeated-sprint ability compared to no re-warm-up during a 15-minute recovery period. Thus, this approach may also be used if it is possible to conduct leg presses in the changing room.

Being well prepared for the second half and starting the second half aggressively may be decisive for the outcome of the match. In a study, match performance with and without re-warm-up at halftime was compared. With re-warm-up, the team had more possession of the ball and less defensive high-intensity running. These findings indicate that re-warm-up at halftime also provides a match advantage at the onset of the second half.

Thus, it is recommended that, after a relaxing period of 6–7 minutes where they may receive tactical information from the coach and partly replenish their muscle glycogen (see Bangsbo 2017),

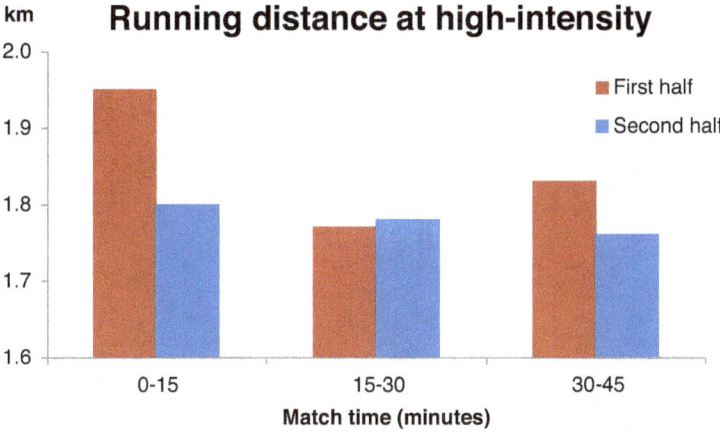

FIGURE 12.1 High-intensity running (>15 km/h) during various periods of a match. Note that the players did less high-intensity running at the start of the second half than in the first half.

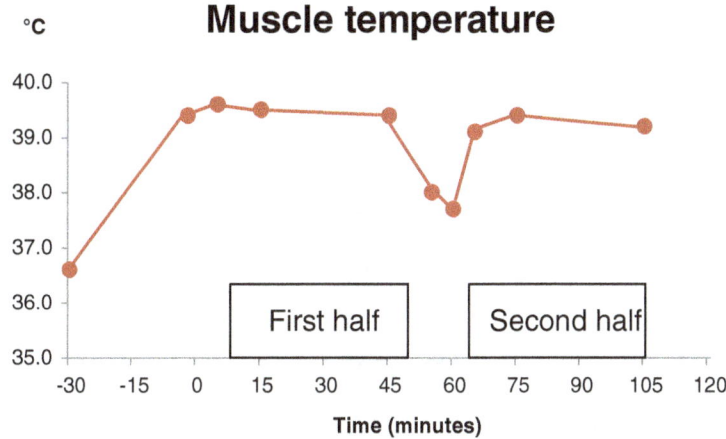

FIGURE 12.2 Muscle temperature before and during a match. Note the marked decrease in muscle temperature at halftime.

the players do some low- and moderate-intensity activities, either in the changing room or on the pitch (see the programs described next).

Programs for Re-warm-up at Halftime

Two programs follow that can be used to regain muscle temperature and improve performance at the start of the second half. One is performed in the changing room and the other on the pitch, which is optimal. However, the coach may prefer to keep the players in the changing room until the start of the second half. For both programs, the intensity of the re-warm-up should be low to moderate in order not to use limited muscle glycogen stores (see Bangsbo 2017).

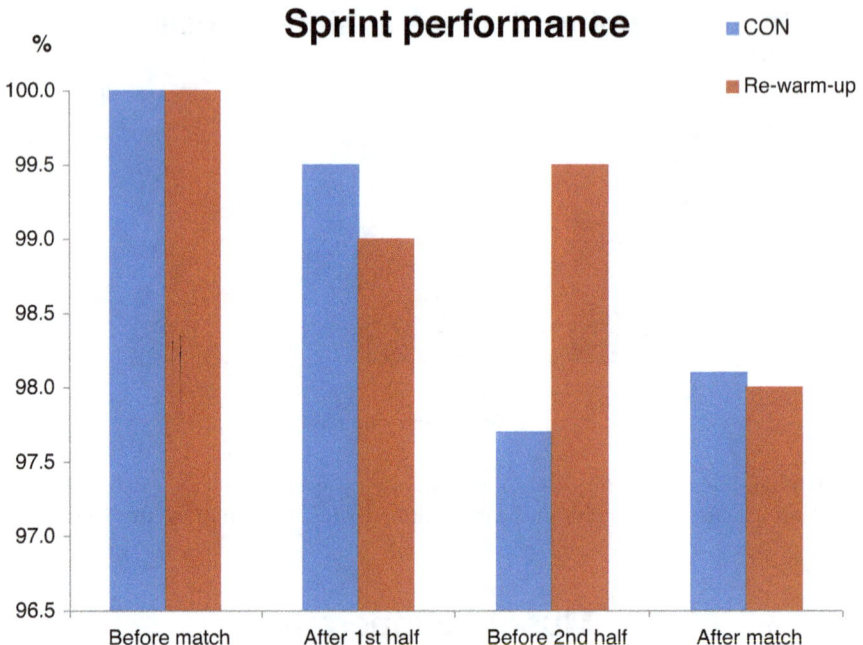

FIGURE 12.3 Sprint performance (average of three 30-meter sprints separated by 30 seconds of recovery) before a match, at the end of the first half, at the start of the second half and at the end of the match with (red bars) or without (blue bars) a re-warm-up program at halftime. The program consisted of 7 minutes of running and activities (average heart rate ≈70% of maximum heart rate). Values are expressed in relation to performance before the match (100%). Note that sprint performance was markedly reduced at halftime with the traditional inactive behavior and is low after the match, whereas with re-warm-up, performance was as good as at the end of the first half.

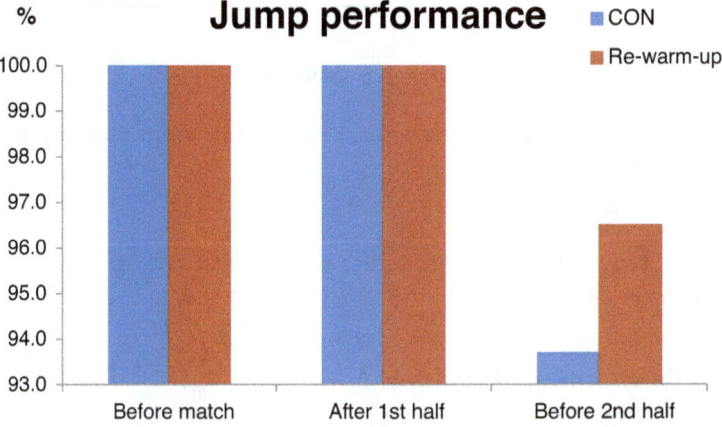

FIGURE 12.4 Countermovement jump performance before a match, at the end of first half and at the start of the second half with (red bars) or without (blue bars) a re-warm-up program at halftime consisting of 7 minutes of running and activities (average heart rate ≈70% of maximum heart rate). Values are expressed in relation to performance before the match (100%). Note that jump performance was markedly reduced during halftime and that the re-warm-up program significantly hindered the reduction.

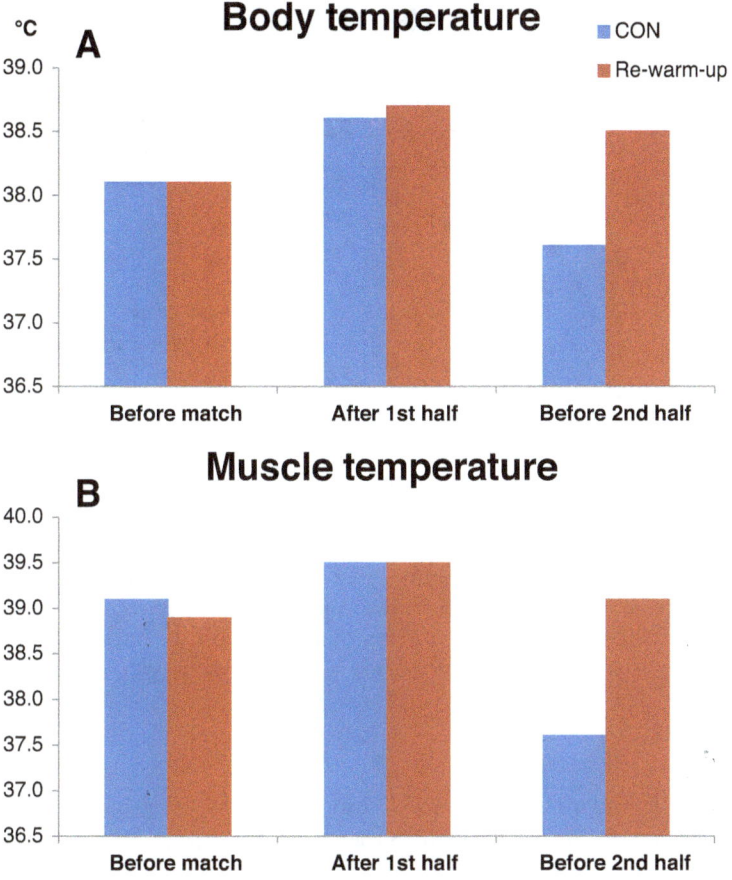

FIGURE 12.5 Body (A) and muscle (B) temperature before a match, at the end of the first half and the start of the second half with (red bars) or without (blue bars) a re-warm-up program at halftime consisting of 7 minutes of running and activities (average heart rate ≈70% of maximum heart rate). Note that the both the body and muscle temperature were markedly higher at the start of second half when re-warm-up was done.

Program 1: Re-warm-up in the Changing Room or Another Indoor Location

0–3 minutes: Dynamic stretching of adductors, abductors and thigh and hamstring muscles (see page 67).
3–6 minutes: Sidestepping, butt kicks and high knees. Each exercise performed twice for 20 seconds.

Program 2: Re-warm-up on the Pitch

0–2 minutes: Jogging.
2–4 minutes: Dynamic stretching exercises for the adductors, abductors and thigh and hamstring muscles (see page 67).

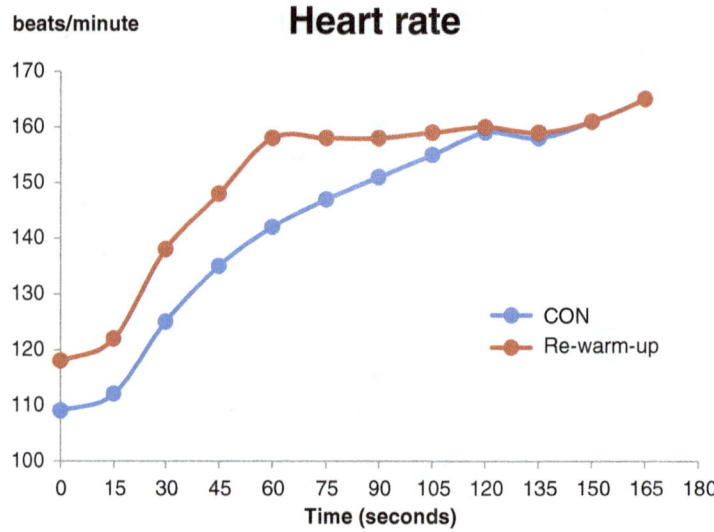

FIGURE 12.6 Heart rate response during the first 3 minutes at the start of the second half with (red) or without (blue) a re-warm-up program at halftime consisting of 7 minutes of running and activities (average heart rate ≈70% of maximum heart rate), which ended 1 minute before the start of the second half. Note that the heart rate increased much faster when the players had done re-warm-up at halftime.

4–7 minutes: Movements with the ball in pairs; change from low to moderate speed running after passing. At the end, perform two 5- to 15-meter sprints.

Re-warm-up Before Extra Time

The time between the end of the match and extra time is officially 5 minutes, but often the rest period is prolonged, and it can be beneficial to do a short re-warm-up program just before the start of extra time to regain muscle temperature. The program should consist of low-intensity exercises in order to not exhaust the players further.

0–2 minutes: Dynamic stretching exercises for the adductors, abductors and thigh and hamstring muscles (see page 67).

Summary

Many teams are not physically prepared for the second half, despite the fact that a re-warm-up period has shown to improve performance. The re-warm-up will increase muscle temperature and should preferably be conducted on the pitch. It should consist of low- to moderate-intensity activities, except for a couple of sprints not longer than 15 meters.

Bibliography

Bangsbo J. *Nutrition in football.* www.soccerfitness.expert, 2017.

Edholm P, Krustrup P, Randers MB. Half-time re-warm up increases performance capacity in male elite soccer players. *Scandinavian Journal of Medicine & Science in Sports* 25: 40–49, 2014.

Lovell R, Midgley A, Barrett S, Carter D, Small K. Effects of different half-time strategies on second half soccer-specific speed, power and dynamic strength. *Scandinavian Journal of Medicine & Science in Sports* 23: 105–113, 2013.

Mohr M, Krustrup P, Bangsbo J. Fatigue in soccer: a brief review. *Journal of Sports Sciences* 23: 593–599, 2005.

Mohr M, Krustrup P, Bangsbo J. Match performance of high-standard soccer players with special reference to development of fatigue. *Journal of Sports Sciences* 21: 519–528, 2003.

Mohr M, Krustrup P, Nybo L, Nielsen JJ, Bangsbo J. Muscle temperature and sprint performance during soccer matches—beneficial effect of re-warm-up at half-time. *Scandinavian Journal of Medicine & Science in Sports* 14: 156–162, 2004.

Zois J, Bishop D, Fairweather I, Ball K, Aughey RJ. High-intensity re-warm-ups enhance soccer performance. *International Journal of Sports Medicine* 34: 800–805, 2013.

13
WARM-UP OF SUBSTITUTES

Depending on competition regulations, between three and an unlimited number of substitutions can be made on either a permanent or rolling basis. Substitutes are typically introduced at halftime or during the second half to minimize the effects of fatigue of players, to alter tactics or to replace underperforming or injured players.

Substitutes cover greater high-intensity running and sprint distances compared to players starting the match and when they start the match over the same period (see Figure 13.1), but they do not perform better compared to when they start the match (see Figure 13.2). Thus, the players seem to be prepared when they enter, but they may be able to perform even better as they only play part of the match. Therefore, it becomes crucial that the substitutes optimize their preparation. One challenge is that the space for warm-up is limited, and another is that it is not always clear when the player will enter the match. Often the coach is uncertain about the optimal time to make the change, and the substitute may have done a complete warm-up and then have to wait a long time before entering the match.

One objective of the warm-up of substitutes is to increase body temperature, as is the case before the match. This requires at least 10 minutes of proper exercises, as described in the following programs. This should be followed by a period where the muscle temperature is maintained until the player enters the match.

An often posed question is whether the substitutes can benefit from preparing before the match. In many teams, substitutes are doing warm-ups alongside the starting 11 players prior to kickoff. However, as the substitutes in most cases spend the majority of the first half seated at the bench, the warming-up effect disappears. The players may feel well after such procedures and there may be a psychological effect of doing exercises before the match, but the activities should be of moderate intensity so as not to use valuable muscle carbohydrate (glycogen) stores. At halftime, the substitutes may perform activities on the pitch and even play a small-sided game (as presented in Program 1), and then maintain the muscle temperature during the second half so they are ready to enter the match. It will also allow them to do some passes and shots on goal. Using such a procedure, however, has the disadvantage that the players may spend too much energy, and it can be challenging for some players to maintain activities during the second half, particularly when there is a limited number of players who are allowed to warm up at the same time (e.g., in many top leagues only three players can warm up at the same time).

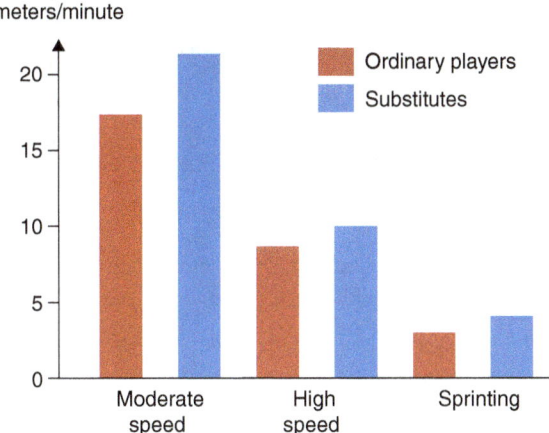

FIGURE 13.1 Mean moderate (14–20 km/h; left), high-speed (20–25 km/h; middle) and sprint (>25 km/h; right) running distance (m/min) of substitutes ("blue") and players performing the entire match ("red") at the same time during the match. Note that the substitutes did more high-speed running than the players completing the entire match.

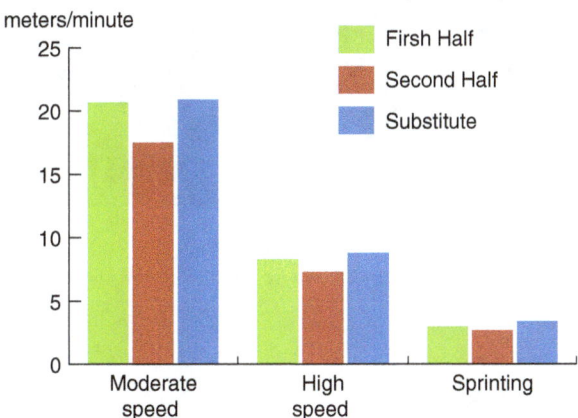

FIGURE 13.2 Mean moderate (14–20 km/h; left), high-speed (20–25 km/h; middle) and sprint (>25 km/h; right) running distance (m/min) of substitutes ("blue") and when the same players started the match (divided into first ("green") and second ("red") halves). Note that the substitutes did more high-speed running when entering the match compared to the second half, but not compared to the first half.

Two programs follow for substitutes, which include periods of movement preparation and exercises to increase body and muscle temperature as well as prepare the muscles for high-intensity actions such as sprinting, jumping and kicking.

The first program begins 5 minutes before the halftime period. It includes a small-sided game to become accustomed to the playing surface and movements of the game, and to prepare the players to enter the pitch at the beginning of the second half or within the first 15 minutes of the second half.

172 Match Preparation

The other program is performed during the match and lasts 15 minutes, followed by a period where muscle and body temperature is maintained. It is recommended when warm-up during the halftime period is not possible.

Program 1: Warm-up of Substitutes During Halftime

0–5 Minutes: Muscle Activation

The aim of the first period is to activate relevant muscles that are used during match play by performing dynamic stretches and using mini-bands to activate glutes, adductors and abductors.

0–2 Minutes: Mini-band Exercises

Wrap the mini-band around the feet or the legs according to the following exercises. All movements should be smooth and controlled.

1. *Lateral walk*: Place the mini-band on the front of the feet and walk sideways while moving in a controlled fashion, avoiding any up-and-down motion. Move in both directions. 30 seconds.

2. *Zig-zag*: Place the mini-band above the ankles and walk in a zig-zag pattern; apply tension on the hips by keeping tension on the band. Move forward, then backward. 30 seconds.

Warm-Up of Substitutes **173**

3. *Squat*: Place the mini-band right below the knees and go to a 90-degree squat position while pressing the knees out in both downward and upward movements. 30 seconds.

2–5 Minutes: Dynamic Stretches

4. *Hip out*: Pull the knee toward the chest and move it to the side as far as possible; lower the leg, working the opposite abductor. 10 repetitions.

5. *Hip in*: Pull the knee out and up, then move it in (while still in the air); lower the leg, working the opposite leg adductor. 10 repetitions.

6. *Forward kick*: Keeping the body straight, perform a forward kick with a straight leg and extended foot. Clapping under the knee will increase the stretch. 10 repetitions.

7. *Forward kick with a twist*: Keeping the body straight, perform a forward kick with a twist. 10 repetitions.

176 Match Preparation

8. *Leg extension stretch*: Move the knee toward the chest and kick the leg out and down. 10 repetitions.

9. *Insides*: Keeping the body and leg straight, kick the leg to the side. 10 repetitions.

10. *Hips*: Keeping the body and leg straight, kick the leg back and pull the opposite arm toward the back leg. 10 repetitions.

5–9 Minutes: Activities and Running

Activities and running are interspersed. Activities are carried out while moving from one side of the pitch to midway, and running is performed from midway to the other side of the pitch (see Figure 13.3).

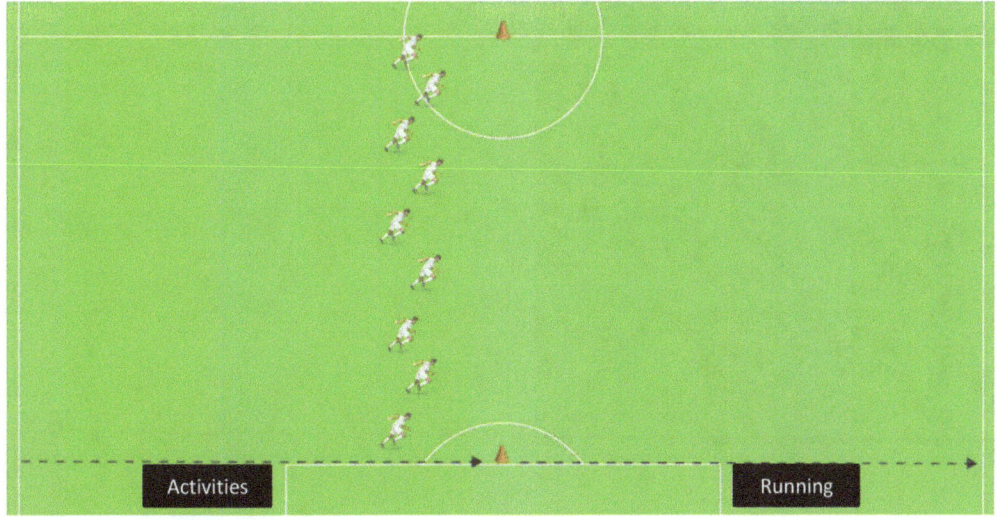

FIGURE 13.3 Activities and running.

11. *Butt kicks*: Heels touch the glutes; arms move in the same way as when running.

12. *High knees*: Move the knees to the horizontal, one at a time.

13. *Skips*: Pull the knee toward the chest; use arms actively to contribute to each skip.

14. *Fast feet forward*: Make quick and short movements of the feet, moving in a zig-zag pattern.

15. *Backward running*: Run backward; look over the shoulder to orientate.

16. *Backward slalom*: Run backward while slaloming; look over the shoulder to orientate.

17. *Fast feet backward*: Same as "fast feet," but backward; look over the shoulder to orientate.

18. *Sidesteps*: Move sideways with a low center of gravity. Change sides after 3 repetitions.

19. *Headers*: Perform jumps for a pretend header, alternating between jumps on right, left and both legs.

20. *Lightning accelerations*: Accelerate forward 5 meters, decelerate and take 2–3 steps backward, then accelerate forward 5 meters.

9–15 Minutes: Small-sided Game

A small-sided game played in a space of 20 m × 15 m. Game is 2 vs. 2 with 2 players placed at each end of the pitch. The players are playing 4 × 1 minute, separated by 30 seconds of rest.

15–17 Minutes: Sprinting

Sprints are performed only if the player enters the match at the start of the second half. This is to ensure neuromuscular activation of (primarily) quadriceps, hamstrings and glutes that are active during high-intensity efforts in football. Four sprints of 10–30 meters are performed, with 30 seconds of recovery between the sprints.

Program 2: Warm-up of Substitutes During the Match

0–5 Minutes: Muscle Activation

The aim of this period is to activate relevant muscles that are used during match play by performing dynamic stretches and using mini-bands to activate glutes, adductors and abductors.

0–2 Minutes: Mini-band Exercises

Wrap the mini-band around the feet or the legs according to the following exercises. All movements should be smooth and controlled.

1. *Tap the floor.* Place the mini-band above the ankles and tap the surface to the side, to the back and in between. The support leg is slightly bent but does not move otherwise. 30 seconds on each leg.

2. *Balance jumps*: Place the mini-band above the ankles and do a set of jumps in different directions. Do two small jumps and one big jump for each set, and keep tension on the mini-band throughout. 30 seconds.

3. *Squat*: Place the mini-band right below the knees and go to a 90-degree squat position while pressing out the knees in both downward and upward movements. 30 seconds.

2–5 Minutes: Dynamic Stretches

4. *Hip out*: Pull the knee toward the chest and move it to the side as far as possible; lower the leg, working the opposite abductor. 10 repetitions.

5. *Hip In*: Pull the knee out and up, then move it in (while still in the air); lower the leg, working the opposite leg adductor. 10 repetitions.

6. *Forward kick*: Keeping the body straight, perform a forward kick with a straight leg and extended foot. Clapping under the knee will increase the stretch. 10 repetitions.

7. *Forward kick with a twist*: Keeping the body straight, perform a forward kick with a twist. 10 repetitions.

Warm-Up of Substitutes **189**

8. *Leg extension stretch*: Move the knee toward the chest and kick the leg out and down. 10 repetitions.

9. *Insides*: Keeping the body and leg straight, kick to the side. 10 repetitions.

10. *Hips*: Keeping the body and leg straight, pull the opposite arm toward the back leg. 10 repetitions.

5–11 Minutes: Activities and Running

The aim of this period is to gradually increase heart rate to 85%–90% of maximum, as this will lead to an increase in body and muscle temperature. Running is combined with various activities.

Players run from the goal line to the technical area at high speed (maximum 10 seconds) with various activities performed on the way back to the goal line (lasting not more than 30 seconds). Runs are repeated twice, and the players should aim at reaching 75% of maximum speed for the first two runs, then 80% for the next two runs, and so on until they reach 95% of maximum running speed (i.e., 10 runs in total). The activities when moving back to the goal line are as follows.

11. *Butt kicks*: Heels touch the glutes; move arms in the same way as when running.

12. *High knees*: Move the knees to horizontal, one at a time.

13. *Skips*: Pull the knee to the chest; use arms actively to contribute to each skip.

14. *Fast feet forward*: Make quick and short movements of the feet, moving in a zig-zag pattern.

15. *Backward running*: Run backward; look over the shoulder to orientate.

16. *Backward slalom*: Run backward while slaloming; look over the shoulder to orientate.

17. *Fast feet backward*: Same as "fast feet," but backward; look over the shoulder to orientate.

18. *Sidesteps*: Move sideways with a low center of gravity. Change sides after 3 repetitions.

19. *Headers*: Perform jumps for a pretend header, alternating between jumps on right, left and both legs.

20. *Lightning acceleration*: Accelerate forward 5 meters, decelerate and take 2–3 steps backward, then accelerate forward 5 meters.

21. *Double shuffle acceleration*: Quickly shuffle to the left and right, followed by a 5-meter acceleration in the direction of the initial shuffles.

11–13 Minutes: Sprinting

To ensure neuromuscular activation of (primarily) quadriceps, hamstrings and glutes that are active during high-intensity efforts in football, perform four sprints of 10–30 meters, with 30 seconds of recovery between the sprints.

Maintenance of Muscle and Body Temperature Until Substitution

The maintenance period is the time between completing the preceding warm-ups and entering the pitch. The aim of this period is to maintain the elevated body and muscle temperature. The players should do this by a sequence consisting of squats, high knees, butt kicks and a couple of jumps every 2 minutes to maintain the augmented body temperature. These activities are interspersed by running from the technical area to the goal line and back at a moderate intensity.

Summary

Substitutes are expected to exceed the physical performance of the players that started the match, therefore it is important that the warm-up of substitutes is sufficient so that the players avoid using precious match time to reach the right body temperature. On the other hand, the warm-up should not be too intense, as it may create temporal fatigue immediately prior to the substitute entering the pitch, thus impairing performance.

Bibliography

Bradley PS, Lago-Peñas C, Rey E. Evaluation of the match performances of substitution players in elite soccer. *International Journal of Sports Physiology and Performance* 9: 415–424, 2014.

Carling C, Espié V, Le Gall F, Bloomfield J, Jullien H. Work-rate of substitutes in elite soccer: a preliminary study. *Journal of Science and Medicine in Sport* 13: 253–255, 2010.

Edholm P, Krustrup P, Randers MB. Half-time re-warm up increases performance capacity in male elite soccer players. *Scandinavian Journal of Medicine & Science in Sports* 25: e40–e49, 2015.

Hills SP, Barwood MJ, Radcliffe JN, Cooke CB, Kilduff LP, Cook CJ, Russell M. Profiling the responses of soccer substitutes: a review of current literature. *Sports Medicine* 48: 2255–2269, 2018.

McGowan CJ, Pyne DB, Thompson KG, Rattray B. Warm-up strategies for sport and exercise: mechanisms and applications. *Sports Medicine* 45, 11: 1523–1546, 2015.

Myers BR. A proposed decision rule for the timing of soccer substitutions. *Journal of Quantitative Analysis in Sports* 8, 1: 1–24, 2012.

Russell M, West DJ, Briggs MA, Bracken RM, Cook CJ, Giroud T, Gill N, Kilduff LP. A passive heat maintenance strategy implemented during a simulated half-time improves lower body power output and repeated sprint ability in professional rugby union players. *PLoS One* 10, 3: e0119374, 2015.

Silva LM, Neiva HP, Marques MC, Izquierdo M, Marinho DA. Effects of warm-up, post-warm-up, and re-warm-up strategies on explosive efforts in team sports: a systematic review. *Sports Medicine* 48, 10: 2285–2299, 2018.

Zois J, Bishop D, Fairweather I, Ball K, Aughey RJ. High-intensity re-warm-ups enhance soccer performance. *International Journal of Sports Medicine* 34: 800–805, 2013.

INDEX

abdominal stretch 64
abductor leg lift 62
accelerations:
    double shuffle 198
    female players 30
    lightning 183, 197
    speed training 126
active bridge 65
airplane 47, 76, 118
air squats 6, 131, 153, 157
ankle activation 46
anterior cruciate ligament 14
arrowhead agility test 140

back:
    kick 26
    stretch 62
backward sprinting 128
backward:
    butt kicks 56, 123, 150
    high knees 56, 124, 150
    running 28, 55, 158, 180, 193
    shuffles 28
    slalom 56, 124, 151, 180, 193
    sprints 59
balance 14, 75
balance jump 185
ball squeeze 50
ballistic stretching 9
ballistic-style preloading activities 161
blizzard survival jacket 159
blood lactate 7
body temperature 5 170, 200
bounding run 22
bridge 50, 80

broad jumps 79, 119
butt-kicks 6, 26, 54, 122, 147, 178, 191

calf stretch 64
carioca 27
catch 108
center circle warm-up 26
circling 15–16
circuit 35
clam 63
collaboration program 85, 86
combination stretch 66, 129
concentric contraction 12
contact jump 80
controlled dynamic stretching 9
cooling 160
coordination 14
core activation 48, 49
countermovement jump 6
countermovement jump test 140
couples program 86, 87
creative speed test 140
cross program 100, 102
curved sprint test 139
cuts 30
cycle ergometer 5

dead lifts 161
decelerations 127
double shuffle acceleration 198
drop jump 161

eccentric contraction 12
environment temperature 11
ergometer:

cycling 129
rowing 129
extra time – warm-up 168

fast feet:
    backward 57, 124, 149, 181, 194
    forward 55, 123, 148, 179, 192
fast running 22
female players 24
five-jump test 140
foam rolling 42
forward
    kick 72, 152, 175, 188;
    with twist 73, 152, 175, 188
front to back 134

garments 159
glute activation 42
glute bridge 48
glutes 70, 117, 121
glycogen 145
go-stop-go 31

half-time warm-up 165, *177*
    indoor 167
    pitch 167
hamstring activation 50
hamstring stretch 61
hamstrings 116
header 58
heading ball 110
heart rate 10, *64, 68*
high kick 26
high knees 6, 27, 54, 122, 136, 147, 159, 178, 191
high-speed running 38, 85
hip activation 42, 49
hip rotation 60
hit the ball 34
hit the cone 33

injuries 8
insides 74, 116, 121, 176, 189
isometric contraction 12, *13*

juggling 84
jumps 21

kick with twist 26
knee to chest 25
kneeling superman 49

lateral:
    kick 25, 153
    movement 135
    shuffles 27
    walk 43, 172
leg:
    extension stretch 73, 121, 152, 176, 189;
    lift 64

lightning:
    accelerations 183, 197
    sprints 59
line program 88
linear sprint test 139
lunges:
    jumping 29–30, 132, 154
    step 118
    walking 77
    walking backward 47
    walking forward 28
lying superman 50

mini-band 42, 172, 184
mountain climber 133
muscle 12
muscle temperature 5, 200

neuromuscular activation 145, 199
non-exhaustive yo-yo intermittent tests 139
nordic:
    hamstring 18, 51, 81
    walk 48, 75, 117, 130

olympic lifts 161

pairs program 83
pendulum 63
plank 17, 49
position-specific warm-up 155
post-activation potentiation 161
power training 129
pre-activation 42, 49
pulled muscle 8
push-up 82, 133
push-up plank 49

quadriceps activation 50
quick run 16

reach 44
repetition maximum 5, 7
resistance 161
reverse nordic 51
rope skipping 129

scarecrow 46
scissor sit-up 81
scorpion 63
self-massage technique 42
short dribbling test 140
sidestep 57, 125, 151, 159, 182, 195
skip 27, 55, 123, 148, 159, 179, 192
small-sided game warm-up 7
speed training 122
square program 91, 92
squat jump 29, 78, 119, 131, 153
squats 20, 44, 51, 76, 119, 161, 173, 186

stair-climbing 129
star jump 22, 46
static stretching 8, 70, 71, 116
step lunge 118
stiffness 8
strength 80
stretching 8
substitute warm-up 190
sumo squat 68, 118, 130

t ankle jump 77
tactical training 10
tap the floor 184
team warm-up 146
thermal comfort 160

three colors 113
thumbs up 49, 81
touch football 111
triangle program 94, 95

u back-lift 158
upper body activation 49

warm-up without ball 54, 67, 82

y program 99
youth players 35
yo-yo intermittent tests 138

zorro sprints 59, 128

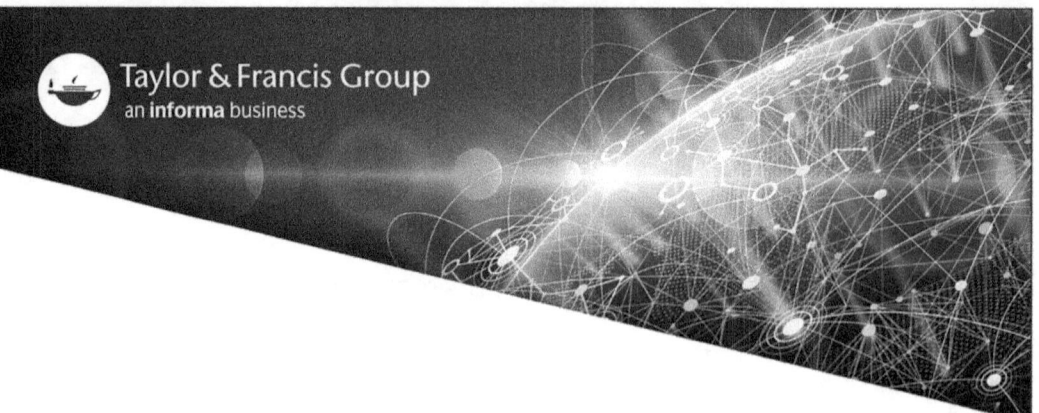

Taylor & Francis eBooks

www.taylorfrancis.com

A single destination for eBooks from Taylor & Francis with increased functionality and an improved user experience to meet the needs of our customers.

90,000+ eBooks of award-winning academic content in Humanities, Social Science, Science, Technology, Engineering, and Medical written by a global network of editors and authors.

TAYLOR & FRANCIS EBOOKS OFFERS:

A streamlined experience for our library customers

A single point of discovery for all of our eBook content

Improved search and discovery of content at both book and chapter level

REQUEST A FREE TRIAL
support@taylorfrancis.com

For Product Safety Concerns and Information please contact our EU
representative GPSR@taylorandfrancis.com
Taylor & Francis Verlag GmbH, Kaufingerstraße 24, 80331 München, Germany